AUTHOR OF
HEROIC LEADERSHIP

JIM DAVIS

PATRIOTIC
LEADERSHIP

TIMELESS WISDOM FROM
NINE PATRIOTS WHO HELPED
FUEL THE AMERICAN SPIRIT

Cover design: Ultimate World Publishing
Layout and typesetting: Ultimate World Publishing
Editor: Marnae Kelley

ULTIMATE WORLD PUBLISHING

Ultimate World Publishing
Diamond Creek,
Victoria Australia 3089
www.writeabook.com.au

Dedication

To all the many brave individuals who have lived, and died, for love of country.

May their courage, innovation, and dedication to freedom and unity continue to inspire us all.

Contents

Introduction	1
Author's Note	3
Chapter One: Samuel Adams –	
American Revolutionary	7
★ *Inauspicious Beginnings*	8
★ *Finding His Voice*	10
★ *The Spark of Influence*	11
★ *Finding Your Voice*	13
★ *Voice Amplified by Passion*	14
★ *Voice Can Take Many Forms*	15
★ *Committees of Correspondence*	16
★ *Don't Raise Your Voice—Strengthen Your Argument*	17
★ *Voice Must Be Guided by Truth*	19
★ *Voices Carry*	20
Chapter Two: Theodore Roosevelt –	
American President	25
★ *A Victor, Not a Victim*	26
★ *Taking Initiative*	28
★ *Why Initiative Matters*	29
★ *But Someone Must Take the Initiative*	30
★ *What Limits Initiative?*	31
★ *What Drives Initiative?*	33
★ *Where Does Initiative Emerge?*	37

★ *Roosevelt, the Life*   38
★ *Roosevelt and the Presidency*   39

Chapter Three: Henry Ford – American Industrialist   **43**

★ *The Start of Something Big*   45
★ *Vision and What Ought to Be*   46
★ *The Catalyst*   47
★ *The People's Entrepreneur*   48
★ *The Beloved Model T*   49
★ *One Thing Leads to Another: The Assembly Line*   52
★ *Success Creates Opportunity*   53
★ *Ford's Leadership Legacy*   54
★ *The Power of Visionary Action*   55
★ *The Ford Family of Employees*   56
★ *Pioneering Industrialist*   57

Chapter Four: George Patton – American General   **61**

★ *An Unwelcomed War*   62
★ *War Demands Warriors*   63
★ *Grace and Accidents*   65
★ *A New and Distinctive Saber for the U.S. Cavalry*   66
★ *Words That Cut Deep*   68
★ *Border Patrol*   69
★ *You Are Here for Three Reasons*   72
★ *War Needs a Reason*   72
★ *You Are Here to Defend Your Homes and Your Loved Ones*   73
★ *You Are Here for Your Own Self-Respect*   74
★ *You Are Real Men*   74
★ *Americans Love a Winner*   75
★ *You Are Not All Going to Die*   75
★ *Legacy*   76

Chapter Five: John Wayne – American Actor ... 81

★ *Character Over Celebrity* ... *83*
★ *Rugged Individualism* ... *85*
★ *Code of the West* ... *87*
★ *Why the Cowboy Code Matters* ... *88*
★ *Essentials from the Code of the West* ... *89*

Chapter Six: Michael Jordan – American Athlete ... 99

★ *An American Sportsman for an American Sport* ... *101*
★ *Not Making the Cut* ... *102*
★ *Blooming Where Planted* ... *103*
★ *Coaching All-Star Potential* ... *104*
★ *Fifteen Seconds* ... *106*
★ *Changing the NBA* ... *107*
★ *Playing Sick* ... *109*
★ *Leadership On and Off the Court* ... *110*
★ *Hard Work* ... *110*
★ *The Value of Team* ... *111*
★ *A Now Focus* ... *112*

Chapter Seven: Amelia Earhart – American Aviator ... 115

★ *Climbing Trees—Made for Adventure* ... *117*
★ *"Flying" Down a Ramp* ... *117*
★ *The First Encounter and Beyond* ... *118*
★ *Pushing Boundaries* ... *120*
★ *More Records and Transatlantic Flights* ... *120*
★ *That Courage Tested* ... *123*
★ *Mastery and Mystery* ... *125*
★ *A Vanished Legend* ... *126*

Chapter Eight: Mark Twain – American Author ... 131

★ *Southern Roots* 132
★ *A Different Kind of Schooling* 133
★ *The Art of Storytelling* 133
★ *Answering the Call* 134
★ *Against the Grain* 135
★ *A Frog and a Leap Forward* 136
★ *Iconic Twain* 137
★ *Fence Painting and Profit* 138
★ *Morality and Conscience* 139
★ *The Mighty Mississippi and Character* 139
★ *American Paradox: Leadership in a Complex Nation* 140
★ *The Conscience of the Nation* 141
★ *Legacy for Modern Leaders* 141
★ *Quips and Quotes* 142
★ *Leading with Laughter and Scorn* 145

Chapter Nine: Harriet Tubman –
American Crusader **149**
★ *Beginning in Bondage* 151
★ *Inspired by a Freer World* 153
★ *Run to the Rescue* 154
★ *Fear* 156
★ *Empathy* 156
★ *Guilt* 157
★ *Anger* 158
★ *Religious Conviction* 158
★ *A Path That Preceded* 159
★ *Unsung Heroes of the Underground Railroad* 160
★ *Moral Leadership in Action* 161

Epilogue: Extending the Legacy More
Leaders Who Defined a Nation **165**
Bibliography **171**
About the Author **177**

Introduction

Stories.

Stories can shape us. They do shape us. They can teach us and inspire us to be better.

The story of America is rich in individuals who not only fueled the spirit of freedom and liberty but formed our nation's history and identity by demonstrating what it truly means to love one's country.

Their lives go beyond mere achievement. They provide enduring lessons in leadership that still remain relevant today.

In these pages, you'll meet nine remarkable Americans whose legacy and impact continue to echo through time.

Sam Adams, who ignited the flames of liberty and revolution through his compelling and persuasive voice; Theodore Roosevelt, who, before assuming the office of president, charged up San Juan Hill with fierce bravery; and Harriet Tubman, risking her life, many times over, to guide her loved ones and others to freedom.

Each embodies a different aspect of patriotic leadership.

But they were all leaders. And they were all proud Americans.

None of these people were perfect. Far from it. Their lives were flawed and rife with mistakes.

1

However, they all shared an unwavering devotion to the American idea and displayed a willingness and ability to act on those deep-seated beliefs and convictions, many times at a high and personal cost.

What makes their lives significant goes far beyond their abilities, accomplishments, and accolades. It is how they used their platforms and influence to serve a cause bigger than themselves.

They more than understood that true devotion isn't blind. It involves the courage to help your country live up to its greatest values and highest aims.

These testaments also remind us that leadership goes beyond position and title. Leadership is about impact and influence. Leadership recognizes a need and musters the courage and moral fortitude to meet it, often when the path is not entirely clear.

As you read the accounts of these nine individuals, you'll discover that patriotic leadership can take on many forms and speak using different tones. It might rumble like George Patton rallying his troops. Other times it might flow from Mark Twain's pen, revealing uncomfortable truths to the world.

But in each case, their brand of leadership serves to move us closer to the America she was always destined to be, rooted in truth, justice, and liberty for all.

This book is more than basic history. The past can point to possibility. All of these patriots show us what we can be and achieve when love for country is combined with a willingness and strength to act and serve others.

Their example continues to help light a way forward, challenging us to continue to write our own chapter and best lives in this story of America that is not yet complete.

How those pages will continue to be filled is still an open book.

Author's Note

"America is not just a country, it's an idea."

—Bono

This is the story of America. The story of the U.S. The story of us.

Included in the following pages is just part of that story.

But it's more than that. Maybe story is not the most apt word to describe what is still a young and short life of what patriotic souls affectionately describe as the *greatest country in the world.*

What defines a patriot today? Abraham Lincoln provides a compelling definition...

"I like to see a man proud of the place in which he lives. I like to see a man live so that his place will be proud of him."

That would seem to be an excellent description of patriotism.

Pride acknowledges past scars and current troubles but also sees the potential for beauty and glory. Pride recognizes that any group, or person, can rise from darkened ashes and still be beautiful and, perhaps, even glorious.

At a time when being extremely proud of one's country is at an all-time low (45 percent) according to Gallup, something certainly seems to have shifted with the populace.*

---

* Gallup

3

A healthy contextual pride in one's nation of birth, or of adoption, creates opportunity to add value to its ethos and culture.

What benefits any community when a major part of the group falls into an attitude of disenchantment regarding the spirit of America many still hold dear?

Add to that a political landscape that is not only extremely divided, but often violently so, and more than just apathy can set in.

Can this be why the United States is morphing into a country that seems to have lost much of its nationalistic spirit? Being a good patriot does not require that an entire citizenry mutually or completely agree. In truth, disagreements and diversity of thought can be a source of growth when tethered to foundational principles and truth.

What of the value of taking pride in your nation of origin?

I have never questioned my gratitude for being born in America, nor have I apologized for her, despite her often dubious moments. Of course, no past is spotless.

Loving your country does not require its perfection.

From where, then, do true patriots derive their sense of pride and devotion? On what do they focus to experience a sense of admiration for what can be appreciated about their people and their country?

The answers define and exemplify those who would be known by that term, *patriots*. They are individuals who love and support the land they lovingly call home.

Can one do that and still find disparity? A casual glance at the relatively brief history of the United States will reveal that answer.

Absolute agreement is not a prerequisite for unity.

The soldier on the battlefield doesn't have to like or embrace everything about the person, or people, he or she is fighting for. That would hinder or prevent the willingness to sacrifice, if needed, their life for that of another.

Thousands of defenders have done so, and continue to, for millions of their fellow citizens.

Presidents will never receive the vote and confidence of *every* American. But the honest ones, genuinely interested in serving the general interests of the office, will work for the good of all, knowing that dissent will always be present.

Doctors, firefighters, police officers, nurses, in every urgent moment, will not wait for certain political winds to blow or ideological stars to align before a rescue.

This sense of unity can be most evident in times of crisis. Remember September 11, 2001, as an emboldened enemy, through horrific acts, had designs to terrorize and weaken America.

It can be argued that the opposite transpired. Scenes of strangers lending a hand to other strangers flooded the landscape.

Why?

Because they were not truly strangers. They, we, were all fellow Americans.

That's the kind of spirit that not only shapes a keen sense of brotherhood, but inspired historic exploits and adventure throughout America's birth, growth, and expansion as a nation.

There has to be something to this idea of patriotism and love of country.

That's why I wrote this book. I share an unabashed pride in our country that so many have had in the past and many do even now.

Can one demonstrate that level of devotion and still acknowledge the many mistakes and errors along the way?

Honesty demands a resounding *yes*. Both patriotism and careful examination can exist in the heart of the devoted patriot and have for generations.

Absolute agreement is not a prerequisite for unity.

My aim in the following chapters is to profile individuals that even the casual reader could recognize who not only kept this fervor and spirit alive, but ultimately became a vital thread in the red, white, and blue fabric of the American story.

Their contributions made an indelible mark and helped change the lives of thousands, if not millions, not just nationally, but globally, and for all time.

I chose to author this book because there is much of which to be proud, much we can learn, and much we can still apply in order to keep the heartbeat of America strong and a resurgence of true patriotic leadership.

It's not about slogans or clichés. It's not even about fruitless debates or contrasting opinions.

It's about caring action.

My hope is, as you read, that will become clear, in full color, and you will be inspired to be a part of what's *best* about America.

That's patriotic leadership.

Read with an open mind and heart and rediscover what these faithful Americans, past and present, can teach us about fueling and keeping it alive and well.

Chapter One

Samuel Adams – American Revolutionary

"It does not take a majority to prevail... but rather an irate, tireless minority, keen on setting brushfires of freedom in the minds of men."

—Samuel Adams

May as well start at the beginning.

There are names strikingly synonymous with the founding of America: Jefferson, Washington, Franklin, Henry, Madison, and more.

Though small in stature, Samuel Adams' also looms large in the story of the genesis and birth of the United States.

Some would even say without him, there would have *been* no founding of America or revolution at all. Whether or not that's an extreme opinion, his significance and renowned place in history is more than secure.

Like his second cousin, John, Sam Adams was instrumental, though by different means, in leading the way and opening the door for the colonists to seek to break away and pursue independence from the tyranny of King George and, by extension, Great Britain.

Samuel Adams was a thorn in the side of the British in the years before the American Revolution. As a political activist and state legislator, he spoke out against British efforts to tax the colonists and pressured merchants to boycott British products.*

And while the past remembers the successful, complete contributions this effective politician made to the birthing of a nation, the tales of his prior career and employment are marked by mediocrity, at best, and, at worst, what many would consider failure.

This is important to note, as professional collapses are not necessarily fatal for any leader or individual. The call to a worthy and life-changing cause can pluck someone from any corner and use him or her to achieve greatness.

The eventual life of Samuel Adams America would come to know, therefore, could be described as an answer to the beckoning of freedom itself.

The story of this central figure in revolutionary history can shed light on how he became possessed by the spirit of many predating the American Revolution, driven by a vision for liberty at all costs.

Inauspicious Beginnings

A graduate of Harvard College, after attending Boston Latin School, Adams was initially unclear regarding his career path. This is not an unusual sensation for any alumnus as they face the world while troubled by thoughts of an uncertain future.

But always, his interest leaned towards politics.

As historian Mark Miller notes, Adams' early business failures would later influence his political ideology, particularly

---

* www.history.com

his distrust of merchant elites and British commercial interests.**

After briefly pondering the idea of entering the legal profession, Adams was hired at a counting house, where financial records were stored. Unfortunately, this was one of multiple jobs at which he failed. He seemed more focused on the political issues of the day, a foreshadowing of things to come.

The position only lasted a few months.

Even with an apparent lack of enthusiasm for the world of business, he accepted a loan from his father to launch an enterprise for himself: 1,000 in sterling or the equivalent of around $23,000 today.

Sadly, he ultimately squandered the money, loaning part of it to a friend and the remainder wasted.

Adams even tried his hand at being a tax collector and wasn't good at that job either, though he did maintain the post for twelve years. He would often fail to collect what was due from various families and eventually found himself 8,000 (of sterling) in the red. Perhaps the fault was not entirely his own. Voice and influence need a proper vehicle and appropriate season.

Purpose thrives best within the right context.

Even during his unexceptional corporate life, Adams found ways to engage his primary passion, politics. While that word may invoke many different, and even negative, thoughts and perspectives these days, Adams saw the arena as a genuine opportunity to ignite change and, yes, spark a revolution.

** Miller, Mark. *The Birth of Modern America: A History, 1619-1939* (Blackwell Publishing, 2006), 92-93.

The call to a worthy and life-changing cause can pluck someone from any corner and use him or her to achieve greatness.

Finding His Voice

Most historians would agree that Adams' emergence as a revolutionary figure began with the Sugar Act, a tax on molasses incoming to the colonists to help pay for administrating land acquired by the British after the French and Indian War.

Clearly this was punitively unjust and unfair to the colonists. Adams was one of many voices to rise in opposition and argue that point.

As Ira Stoll documents in his definitive biography, Adams' response to this act marked his transformation from local politician to revolutionary leader.* As a member of the Town Meeting, a form of government with roots going back to the 1620s, in New England, he took advantage of the opportunity to not only speak against the tax but to rally the thirteen colonies in presenting a unified opposition and resistance to what was clearly an unwarranted levy.

In the following words, written as a letter to the Governor of Massachusetts in 1765, he even compared the situation to the equivalent of being in a type of bondage to the Crown:

> *For if our Trade may be taxed, why not our Lands? Why not the Produce of our Lands & everything we possess or make use of? This we apprehend annihilates our Charter Right to govern & tax ourselves. It strikes at our British privileges, which as we have never forfeited them, we hold in common with our Fellow Subjects who are Natives of Britain. If Taxes are laid upon us in any shape without our having a legal Representation where*

---

* Stoll, Ira. *Samuel Adams: A Life* (Free Press, 2008), 45-47.

they are laid, are we not reduced from the Character of free Subjects to the miserable State of tributary Slaves?**

This clearly contrasts the reality of freedom verses tyranny. The colonist no longer wanted to be a subject and certainly did not want to feel penalized or billed, with prejudice, to support an effort initiated by a country from which they wished to detach.

No doubt Adams' words and perspective mirrored many. Persuasion, however, includes, and often demands, a strong voice.

Revolutionary ideas may start in the mind and the heart but, without capable expression, may die there. Whether it was writing, speaking, or otherwise actively crying out against British tyranny, Adams was an ardent contester and voice to support the burgeoning idea of freedom in the minds of those he influenced.

The Spark of Influence

Adams consistently railed against the unfair treatment of the Colonists by King George, especially in matters of trade.

One such instance was the Tea Act, which was not a tax, but a way to allow the East India Company to forego the import tax and sell using merchants *they* would select, thus creating a monopoly. Adams and others saw this as a scheme to reinforce the already existing duty on tea the Colonists had to pay, to which they never agreed.

On December 16, 1773, Adams spoke out against this practice at a town meeting. Perhaps not coincidentally, that night, men disguised as Native Americans would board three of those import ships, which were sitting in the Boston Harbor, and throw 342 chests of tea overboard.

** Otis, James Jr., *The Rights of the British Colonies Asserted and Proved* (Edes and Gill, 1764), 47-48.

Even the most casual observer of history knows about the Boston Tea Party. Would they have devised that kind of protest had Adams not spoken that night? It's impossible to say without doubt.

Is it more than plausible that his words and argument added to the sway many were already sensing? Of course. That is the *spark of influence* that can ignite a cause or fuel any vision. It is the essence of leadership.

Benjamin Woods Labaree, in his compelling study of the event, maintains that while Adams may not have directly coordinated the destruction of the tea, his address at the Old South Meeting House that afternoon provided the intellectual and moral reason for the action.*

Every history is filled with individuals who lent their voices to causes they believed in and sought to persuade with the power of language. It seems that Adams was not a huge fan of numbers but loved words.

He wouldn't be the first or last.

Leadership is influence and influence is voice. The power of one's argument is found in the artful choice of language. Adams knew this. So did Winston Churchill, Abraham Lincoln, and Dr. Martin Luther King, Jr.

The right words can serve as the exact influence a person or society needs at just the right time. So it was for Adams, and for this time, at America's birth, and throughout her story. The ability to stand up and speak up to inspire others towards a better future is every leader's opportunity and obligation.

That's leadership. That's all it is.

Well, that's not entirely all, but it certainly begins there.

Perhaps Adams did not even see himself as a leader, or insurrectionist, for that matter. Maybe he was simply following

---

* Labaree, Benjamin Woods. *The Boston Tea Party* (Northeastern University Press, 1979), pp. 141-144.

his instincts and allowing them to drive his activity and conduct.

Often, the result of such motives can only be seen *following* certain events, not during the course of them. But that makes speaking up even more important. Better to rise than to wake later knowing you could have said something sooner.

Adams intuitively recognized this and seemed more than happy and content to step into the forefront of resisting the totalitarianism being dictated from England.

Finding Your Voice

What drives passion? What motivates? Whatever that is will fill conversation and flood the mind with better visions of the future.

One can't discount or underestimate the power of cause when it comes to the desire to voice a plea, concern, or even engage in confrontation. Variance in that regard doesn't reduce the significance of why one acts or seeks to influence. It only provides other colors and shades.

Voice Amplified by Passion

A message, for any leader, is either enhanced or diluted based on its level of fervor.

No one is advocating for raving lunacy. But some raving could be in order.

Passion stimulates the hearts and minds of the hearers. It's the fire that ignites. It's the power of the voice that reverberates and provokes ideas and actions far beyond the norm. Adams and his counterparts perfected this. Through his writings and his speeches, his words dripped in fury, not in an odious way, but visionary, almost prophetic.

If voice is influence, there are many layers to that maxim. In other words, this principle is simple, not simplistic. Simple is easy to understand. Simplistic is shallow. The parallel between leadership and influence is both simple and very deep.

Whether or not Adams saw himself in the light of a visionary leader, history certainly does. As Richard D. Brown observes, Adams' genius lay in his ability to combine passionate rhetoric with practical organization, making him the most successful political organizer and propagandist in American history before the modern era.*

There is no vision without *passion*. No one is going to be excited about a boring message or a second-rate campaign. There are truly too many roaring flames for onlookers to be attracted to small sparks.

Social media has done modern society no favors. There was a time the written word carried much weight given the care of thought and the time invested to compose.

Now, with just a few keystrokes, a mass of thoughts and opinions flood the internet, muddying the whole idea of what's

---

* Brown, Richard D. *Revolutionary Politics in Massachusetts: The Boston Committee of Correspondence and the Towns, 1772-1774* (Harvard University Press, 1970), 58.

profoundly important and worthy of conversation, much less any kind of active involvement.

Not every argument is viable. Not every message has actual value.

There is no vision without passion. No one is going to be excited about a boring message or a second-rate campaign.

History validates the contention Adams and the Founding Fathers had with Great Britain and King George. Their words are still read and honored today because of the import they carried and the passion that was behind every one of them.

Voice Can Take Many Forms

"Let us dare to read, think, speak, and write." —Sam Adams

Technology has afforded the world many more ways to use one's voice. Perhaps, to a large degree, too many. Clearly this was not the case in Adams' day. Methods of communication were much more rudimentary, slow, and deliberate. Often the news could be considered old by the time one was able to read it!

However, that was not to say that activists did not work hard to employ as many means as necessary to spread the word and bolster their campaign. Channels such as letters, sermons, speeches, meetings, pamphlets, newspapers, and magazines were instrumental in disseminating information to as broad an audience as possible given the limitations time and distance presented in that era.

Often these tools were employed in a sequential manner, other times more sporadically, but each was chosen to garner the best possible outcome for the situation. It was not random. It was strategic. It had to be, given the lack of ease that was involved.

Committees of Correspondence

One example from the life and work of Adams was his creation of the Committees of Correspondence. While it could be tempting to easily dismiss the idea of a "committee," there is merit in the brief history of this group.

The Committees of Correspondence, as Pauline Maier demonstrates in her groundbreaking work, represented the first systematic intercolonial communication network in American history.* Through these committees, Adams created what historian Thomas H. O'Connor describes as the first political machine in American history.**

This was no typical set of committees. Granted, that word is often, and fairly understandably, associated with groups who say much but do little due to a bog of bureaucracy or needless procedures. From a leadership perspective, this could actually stifle or belay the kind of results that a voice of passion could, and should, bring.

This was not that. The Committees of Correspondence were provisional governments Adams established in the

---

* Maier, Pauline. *From Resistance to Revolution: Colonial Radicals and the Development of American Opposition to Britain, 1765-1776* (Norton, 1991), 224-227.

** O'Connor, Thomas H. *The Hub: Boston Past and Present* (Northeastern University Press, 2001), 56.

thirteen American colonies. This was a primary way of exchanging ideas, expressing concerns, and promoting designs of a growing movement towards freedom and independence.

Adams also launched a newspaper with his friend called *The Public Advertiser*, yet another vehicle for broadcasting his opinions regarding the current struggle against British tyranny.

Method matters. The strength of a compelling message can frequently be lessened because of the wrong choice of means. Those who lived in the days of pen and ink had to choose wisely which method to employ to best convey their ideas and lead others to join their campaign.

Fast forward over 200 years, the modern leader must be equally selective given the seeming plethora of tools to use.

Communication seems a bit cheap these days. Fast. Easy. Adams understood the supreme power of words and would never allow important truths to be diminished for the sake of convenience or expedience.

As Richard D. Brown observes, Adams' genius lay in his ability to combine passionate rhetoric with practical organization, making him the most successful political organizer and propagandist in American history before the modern era.***

Using the best form for one's best message is paramount.

Don't Raise Your Voice—Strengthen Your Argument

Volume does not equal effective persuasion. While passion and excitement will come through and resonate, shouting should never be a trend, and clamor does not necessarily mean there is a compelling case.

---

* Brown, Richard D. *Revolutionary Politics in Massachusetts: The Boston Committee of Correspondence and the Towns, 1772-1774* (Harvard University Press, 1970), 58.

When the latter occurs, can it be because facts become washed away in a flood of emotion and feelings override reason? No leader with a vision or dream is exempt from resistance. The power in the response and resulting discourse should be wrapped in rationale more than ire.

Clearly Adams experienced this. The rise of a group known as the Anti-Federalists proved that. Handling resistance with logic and rationale was key then, and it is for any argument.

Freedom, and the creation of a strong government dedicated to the people, *would* seem a contrary objective about which to argue, though the journey of any epic change is checkered with comments that can reflect a fear of change that is more phantom than real.

Stepping back, looking at the big picture, that is the test of leadership. Defining truth, focusing on the factual and actual, not the imaginary dragons, and looking ahead to what can be is the prospect of every worthy cause. Without those two hinge points, any case for positive action and change will be diminished.

Adams and his contemporaries deftly compared and contrasted the present certainty of tyranny under King George to the option of living in freedom in an environment that had yet to be created. That's the power of what became revolutionary influence.

Thousands rallied to the cause. More would fight and give their lives to purchase freedom and realize true independence. With the substance of well-chosen words, Adams and his compatriots stirred a generation. No doubt passion was infused. But without a solid basis for the idea, all the roaring Adams could do would not bring the masses any closer to his side.

As historian Robert Middlekauff explains, Adams understood that revolution required not just passion but persuasion, not just anger but argument.*

---

* Middlekauff, Robert. *The Glorious Cause: The American Revolution, 1763-1789* (Oxford University Press, 2005), 233.

Voice Must Be Guided by Truth

With information and communication so readily available at everyone's fingertips, the perception might be that much of it is lined with authenticity or accuracy.

Of course, this is not always the case. For too many so-called thought leaders or influencers, there is often an angle or ulterior motive that replaces honest messaging.

Adams had no need to lie or even embellish the truth about what he considered to be the evil designs of King George. He stated that case emphatically and used it to galvanize his followers to fight for something better.

Truth can be both an activator and a foundation. It's an active agent, in that it can present a need to do something, to advance in defense of an ideal or advance of one.

Truth is a stabilizer. This is exhibited in the many times the Constitution is referred to as the law of the land. These laws were not put in place to confine Americans but to liberate and protect them as citizens.

Even so, various attempts, from time to time, are made in an attempt to diminish, fudge, or even thwart the Constitution and its fundamental principles. While some may agree with the latitude necessary for that kind of mistaken effort, the Founders, and Adams, would certainly not have approved.

These individuals were stalwarts of conviction. Every leader worth his or her salt should commit to vigorously protect and espouse what they believe to be righteous. Anything less is a poor disservice to their platform.

Today, truth can be in short supply and its lack detracts from the preservation of the kind of ideals for which Adams and others fought.

For the leader of any movement, proper guidance demands integrity, and there's no integrity without truth.

Influence demands integrity,
and there's no integrity without truth.

Voices Carry

The reason anyone is still talking about people like Sam Adams and the others that are outlined in this book is because their voice and words transcended time and proceeding generations.

Voices carry. Or at least they can. How messages reverberate, and to what degree, can certainly differ.

Consider the following words and what image and sounds come to mind.

"Four score and seven years ago."

"The only thing we have to fear is fear itself."

"I have a dream."

"Ask not what your country can do for you..."

"Mr. Gorbachev, tear down this wall."

Did Lincoln's troubled face appear along with the sound of his melancholy voice? Was encouragement found in the enthusiastic reinforcement of hope in Roosevelt's speech? What snapshot of past America and the vision of the future materialized when thinking about Martin Luther King's fervent, four-word mantra? Consider the selflessness espoused by Kennedy's challenge to be more motivated by service to country than the other way around.

Remember the seriousness and righteous indignation Reagan embodied when giving the Russian Premiere such a strong directive bathed in the idea of human rights.

Their voices carry today. Why? Because of the stuff and substance that grounded each and every one; they were ignited with the spark of independence and freedom.

The same can be said of Sam Adams and his contemporaries. This "Son of Liberty" is a shining example of how one voice, added to many others, can influence and inspire others to embrace a cause that can lead to powerful moments in history.

Revolution can result in mighty victory but can begin with a small but growing willingness to summon courage and speak up. That's the power of influence. That's voice.

The life of Samuel Adams proves that one person with a strong, true message can make a difference and even help change the course of history. He was able to move past early struggles and challenges in his professional life and rise to become one of the more pivotal figures in the Revolution.

Adams showed where leadership actually exists, not in titles or position, but the moral fortitude to stand up and *speak up* using various means, from livened speeches to the written word, to amplify his voice and galvanize a people towards a movement.

Adam's legacy goes beyond the founding of America, which is obviously significant by itself. His example serves as a reminder that revolutionary change and ideas can begin with a single voice willing to challenge injustice or even indifference. It's also an invitation to strive, in this era of information overload, to weigh our words and judge them by truth, not platitudes or empty bravado.

Injustice still exists. But passion without substance is null and void and will not save the world. There are still those who are "irate" and "tireless," those who can be roused and inspired the same way that Sam Adams did to use *their* voice and use it for serving the greater good.

Leadership is influence and influence is voice. One spark can light a brushfire of change. Adams proved that. And did so in a revolutionary way. His ultimate mission and achievement echoes beyond the battle and birth of a nation.

It teaches that the truth can challenge and seek to overturn prejudice and any apathy towards change.

Adams, like many of his contemporaries, carried a spirit and moral fortitude that, while it led to greater good, was considered radical and rebellious.

All the better, as it sparked a revolution and helped make way for the founding of a nation.

Adams' Leadership Principles

★ **Find Your True Calling:** Adams overcame early professional struggles to become one of the most consequential figures in Revolutionary history. True purpose trumps temporary setbacks.

★ **Lead With Clear Vision:** Adams wasn't just arguing against England's oppressiveness. He articulated a brighter and freer future that inspired others to join the cause.

★ **Use Your Voice to Inspire Change:** Adams didn't just talk about revolution; he motivated others through powerful words and deeds that sparked world-changing action.

★ **Utilize Multiple Communication Channels:** Adams mastered various forms of communication to spread his message, from speeches to pamphlets to committees, proving that leaders must adapt their methods to reach their audience.

★ **Harness the Power of Words:** Empty rhetoric wins few arguments. True strength lies in the substance and authenticity of the message being conveyed.

★ **Anchor Leadership in Truth:** Adams' messaging was grounded in truth and integrity, the essential bedrock of lasting influence and change.

★ **Work for Legacy:** Adams' dedication to liberty would endure beyond his lifetime. His work shows that true leaders build foundations that outlast them.

Chapter Two

Theodore Roosevelt – American President

*"This country will not be a good place for any of us to live in
unless we make it a good place for all of us to live in."*

—Theodore Roosevelt

If there has ever been one individual who personified the
true essence of the American spirit in one body and in one
life, it was Theodore Roosevelt.

He was never supposed to be president, though. The initial
arrangement to make him vice president was made by the bosses
in the New York Republican Party to "move him upstairs" due
to his success at fighting and eliminating corruption both as
governor and, before that, chief of police for the city of New
York.

The idea was to essentially get him out of the way, to reduce
his level of influence and power, and place him in a position
that would be largely useless and hope that McKinley would
"not die" for the next four years.

Otherwise, the office of vice president would be perfectly suited for the person who was either unwilling or unable to make any discernable impact in that role, save assuming the presidency if that would become necessary.

On September 6, 1901, while at the Pan-American Exposition at the Temple of Music in Buffalo, New York, Leon Czolgosz brazenly drew a gun and shot President McKinley twice in a receiving line. The first bullet miraculously ricochets off a suit button and lodges in the folds of the president's jacket. As the gun is fired a second time the round penetrates McKinley's stomach, felling him to the ground.

The president would, indeed, die eight days later. Instantly, a thousand crucial moments culminated, translating into one of the most dynamic and indelible presidencies in American history.

Whether you agree or disagree with the policies of the Roosevelt administration, of which a number of finer points could be argued, few individuals have put their unique stamp on their time in the Oval Office quite like Teddy Roosevelt.

Known as the "Lion in the White House," he was a tenacious, often aggressive, leader who increased America's influence in the world, protected what he viewed as the rights of the populous, and safeguarded many of America's natural lands.

None of this was by accident. He was a man made for his times, and that began as a child.

A Victor, Not a Victim

Remember those thousands of moments that transform into a big moment? For Roosevelt, these were forged with intention, purpose, grit, and determination. Roosevelt would become known as a tireless worker who exemplified the "strenuous life," but that wasn't reflected in his early existence.

Though he was born into relative wealth and ease, that brings little comfort to a child who suffered from malnutrition, due to a lack of appetite, and unpredictable bouts of asthma.

To put it plainly, young Theodore Roosevelt was physically *poor.* The asthma could be so severe that at times he felt he was drowning as he would gasp for air.

"I was a sickly, delicate boy...but I had a wise and far-seeing mother who made me lead an outdoor life... She forced me, even though my heart was heavy, to work and to work hard." *

Though his parents had substantial resources of which to deploy for his care, many of the remedies utilized were suspect. Some of these prescriptions would include electric shock, nearly violent massages, black coffee, and cigar smoking to induce vomiting.

All to little or no avail. Absent viable medical solutions, Roosevelt would better find comfort in the person of his father. Theodore idolized the elder Roosevelt. It was his father who would later tell Theodore that he had the mind but not the body to match, even using the contrarian endearment of "wimp."

He would have to "make" his body, said his father. *"Theodore,"* his father said, sitting on his bed one night, *"you have the mind, but you have not the body, and without the help of the body the mind cannot go as far as it should. You must make your body. It is hard drudgery to make one's body, but I know you will do it."* **

That's a choice. That's a challenge. One that Theodore Roosevelt more than met.

While most people would agree that exercise is important, Roosevelt would push his limits to their extreme, spending

---

* Roosevelt, Theodore. *An Autobiography* (Charles Scribner's Sons, 1913), 18.

** Morris, Edmund. *The Rise of Theodore Roosevelt* (Coward, McCann & Geoghegan, 1979), 61.

hours on gymnastic equipment in an upstairs gymnasium his father converted at the family residence. He also took boxing lessons from a prizefighter and lifted weights.

These early, hearty actions taken by a young man who could have resigned himself to plod along in a weakly body not only proved successful, but would also serve as key ingredients for what would be known and embraced as that strenuous life that would be forever associated with the twenty-sixth president.

This was the victor mentality and fighting spirit would follow and define Roosevelt throughout his life and career and surface in a variety of situations and arenas.

*"Unless we are willing to work to capacity, we have no right to live at all... I determined to be strong and well and did everything to make myself so. By the time I entered Harvard I was able to take my part in whatever sports I liked."**

Taking Initiative

One trait that would come to define Theodore Roosevelt was his willingness to take initiative even in the face of opposition,

---

* Roosevelt, Theodore. *Theodore Roosevelt: An Autobiography.* (Macmillan, 1913), 32.

tradition, or idle bureaucracy. Such was the case as a fledgling assembly member for the state of New York.

His stance and contempt for the unethical would lead to some courageous action for such a fresh, twenty-three-year-old state official (the youngest ever elected), angering many, chief among them, Jay Gould.

While Roosevelt stood for honesty in government, this wealthy but corrupt financier was not averse to colluding with judges to win favors. One of T.R.'s biggest battles came when Gould did so with certain officials, including Judge Theodore Westbrook, in an attempt to get his taxes lowered.

This was an affront to everything which Roosevelt held right and true, including the reason and trust with which he believed he was placed in office. The young assemblyman from the Twenty-first District has displayed a degree of courage that older legislators might well emulate... His attack on Judge Westbrook's dealings with Jay Gould has shaken Albany to its foundations.**

Thus, he did what his heart and instincts directed: he took the lead and challenged the corruption, even as far as to petition Grover Cleveland, governor at the time, to pass a Civil Reform Bill.

Roosevelt would eventually become minority leader, working, and battling inside the machinery of statewide politics. This proved to be a solid proving ground for T.R.'s later years, including, of course, his time in the White House.

Why Initiative Matters

It could be argued that America would not even be an independent and free nation without initiative. As outlined in Chapter One, the bold decision to break from a tyrannical

---

** "Young Roosevelt Takes Stand Against Corruption." *New York Tribune*, April 8, 1882: 2.

king, oppressive taxes, and overall totalitarianism, then fight a brutal, seemingly unwinnable war to start a new country is more than daunting.

But the stronger the reason the stronger the incentive to fight and continue the battle until the dream is realized, or victory is achieved. This is what separates the dreamers and the doers.

Dreams stir imagination; initiative propels forward motion.

As T.E. Lawrence said,

"All men dream: but not equally. Those who dream by night in the dusty recesses of their minds wake up in the day to find it was vanity, but the dreamers of the day are dangerous men, for they may act their dreams with open eyes, to make it possible."

Ideas don't work unless people do. Nothing happens until someone provides leadership or action for it. The founders knew this, and so did Roosevelt.

We might still be paying taxes to an overlording monarch in Great Britain had the likes of Sam Adams, Patrick Henry, Alexander Hamilton, Thomas Jefferson, and George Washington, along with others, not stepped in and stepped *up* with truly credible and courageous inventiveness. That's not to even mention the colonists themselves and their active participation.

Roosevelt would have made a great Founding Father.

But Someone Must Take the Initiative

Two people can see the same problem and have two quite different perspectives. No doubt others saw corruption and the hardship it brought on the residents of New York, but few rose to do much about it. Initiative, as T.R. would agree, puts one in the "arena."

This is why we celebrate and mark the lives of those who aren't waiting to be invited to make a difference. They, indeed, made a change, and initiative was the stimulus.

For leaders, this is crucial. Who wants to follow a lazy or uninspired individual who lacks the drive to act? It would seem counterintuitive to attempt to lead without a sense of enterprise or drive that would seek to create a shift or start something new.

Leaders are in front. At least, that is where they are supposed to be.

In his own words, Roosevelt stated,

"In any moment of decision, the best thing you can do is the right thing, the next best thing is the wrong thing, and the worst thing you can do is nothing." *

Clearly there are barriers, whether psychological or emotional, sometimes physical, that our fellow patriots, throughout the American story, have needed to overcome.

Dreams ignite, initiative fuels forward motion.

What Limits Initiative?

Possessing and taking initiative strikes the balance between knowing one's limitations and the idea that the only real constraints are the ones in the mind placed there voluntarily. Determined leaders understand they are a mixed bag of both strengths and weaknesses and press on anyway when they believe it's the right thing to do.

They don't let the following constraints prevent them from impacting others and implementing viable situations in real and lasting ways.

---

* Roosevelt, Theodore. Address to Harvard University, 1901. Presidential Papers, Library of Congress.

- **Apprehension:** While there are some healthy matters that can cause concern, irrational apprehension is paralyzing. It causes one to stop or shrink back. Hesitation has killed more dreams and potential greatness than any circumstance. Most of what people dread never happens.

- **Doubt:** Like apprehension, doubt can creep into one's mind and cause them to imagine failure before a venture is yet started. Doubt invokes uncertainty. It robs potential victory needlessly.

  Doubt will keep a life small and constricted. Doubt is too small a house in which to live.

- **Resistance:** Amazingly, those who may criticize the most are the ones doing the least. Their arms are folded while the achievers are taking the wheel. Roosevelt, in his famous "Man in the Arena" speech, made it clear that critics don't count. Having said that, resistance can come from well-intentioned people who are simply disinterested in change. Most resist it, even if it's a promising idea and can be good for them.

  It can also exist in the mind of one that resists or rejects change.

- **Complacency:** Why are there many who consistently remain the same while life proceeds like a parade seemingly beyond notice? Where do ruts originate, or the attitude that coasting is preferable to vigorously running and reaching the finish line with gusto? Is it easier to be complacent than driven? Absent a sense of purpose, calling, and an enterprising temperament, the answer is painfully obvious. One must fight against gravity or fall victim to it.

- **Negativity:** The negative mind will set a black cloud over, or put a wooden stake through, any potentially fortunate moment. It's the ultimate downer. For some, it becomes a lifestyle and trend because those are the dominate thoughts that are allowed to dwell in their heads and words from their lips.

Changing the world is challenging enough. One does not need to be wearing the wet blanket of negativity while trying to do it!

What Drives Initiative?

If there are killers of the willingness to step out and be tenacious and action oriented, then there must be internal stimuli that can propel a person forward into potential greatness.

★ **Integrity:** This was a key motivating factor for Roosevelt throughout his personal and professional life. As chief of police, he would scour local bars to extract drunken officers as, clearly, that was not what they were supposed to be doing at the time!

Knowing the right thing, or right things, to do is the starting point that serves as solid ground for a purposeful life of action.

Integrity is acting from a set of guiding principles and doing what's right because it's the right thing to do. For the patriot, such truths that can derive from the Bible, the U.S. Constitution, and even the Magna Carta, have been more than instrumental when properly applied.

★ **Courage:** A life of action is not for the timid. It's not casual, it's *courageous*. Consider the Cowardly Lion. A viewing of that classic 1939 film contains confusing moments when the character who is supposedly the King of the Forest cowers in fear at every turn.

Courage is not the absence of fear, or an act of foolishness. It's not devoid of wisdom or deliberate thought. In fact, the greater the task or mission is, the stronger the state of mind needs to be.

Courage talks to and manages one's emotions, not the other way around. Even so, it's still a summoning of all that the brave spirit can muster.

T.R. demonstrated this while leading his "Rough Riders" up San Juan Hill during the Spanish-American War. He rode up and down the hill on horseback while telling his men to "march" up Kettle Hill. He would lead several such charges an instilled courage and a spirit of victory in the men he led into battle.

★ **Pluck:** Similar to courage, pluck is the desire to continue to fight for what is right against overwhelming or steady opposition. Would a life of taking action and battling rivaling interests travel a calm road?

Far from it.

"I have always had a horror of words that are not translated into deeds, of speech that does not result in action." *

Remember, critics didn't count. As previously mentioned, those who typically have the most to say about the activities of others are the same ones who are doing the least. These do-nothings will be happy to proclaim how it should be done differently from the sidelines. How can individuals not in the "arena," in good conscience, disparage those who are?

All of it carries no weight. Better to persevere and simply consider from where negative chatter derives.

One must outlast his or her critics, not fight them. Let ideas and accomplishments speak for themselves and make the case mere words cannot.

---

* Roosevelt, Theodore. Letter to Henry L. Sprague, January 26, 1900. Presidential Papers, Library of Congress.

★ **Aspiration**: Is there a higher plane where any individual can seek to reach? Of course. It may look different for each person, but the overall motivation should be the same, to keep reaching and moving forward to be more than ever before.

While that may sound pollyannish or like bumper sticker philosophy, aspiration is the perfect antidote for a life of laziness and indifference. Roosevelt knew and pursued this ideal disposition.

"I wish to preach, not the doctrine of ignoble ease, but the doctrine of the strenuous life, the life of toil and effort, of labor and strife; to preach that highest form of success which comes, not to the man who desires mere easy peace, but to the man who does not shrink from danger, from hardship, or from bitter toil, and who out of these wins the splendid ultimate triumph." **

*One must fight against gravity
or fall victim to it.*

The leader will never be able to help others aspire to be more and do more if their personal and professional efforts are stuck in neutral. The best aspirations are grounded in God-given purpose and not to be taken lightly.

The right aspirations can lift everybody higher. That's a big part of what leadership is all about.

★ **Motion**: None of the above matters, or would even be necessary, without the reality of forward motion. It would be like a new car with no engine. It will look nice in the driveway, but it wasn't built to remain parked.

** Roosevelt, Theodore. "The Strenuous Life." Speech at Hamilton Club, Chicago, April 10, 1899. In *The Works of Theodore Roosevelt, Memorial Edition*, Vol. 13, 319-320.

Theodore Roosevelt's life was constant motion, from when he rose, which was early, until he went to bed, which, at 12:00 a.m., was *not*. He was able to pack more in one day than most could in a week.

The President never wasted a moment... He would often say that a person should always aim to make every hour count for something definite, something that moved him forward either mentally, morally, or physically. Mere existence without progress was, to him, inconceivable.*

Why is this important? Because daily agenda matters. Time is an ingredient, and each moment is a window of opportunity and time truly does not wait for anyone. It will ignore and leave the passive behind.

Theodore Roosevelt lived his life on the other side of this reality, recognizing that time could be his ally and there was no time for standing still. There was too much good he wanted to do. There was far too much potential impact to allow a moment to remain dormant or unused.

Life is movement. Idle existence breeds stagnation. Initiative requires propellent. Forward is not only a direction. It's an attitude.

---

* Loeb, William Jr. *Personal Memories of Theodore Roosevelt.* Unpublished manuscript, 1922. Theodore Roosevelt Collection, Harvard University Library, 47.

Where Does Initiative Emerge?

The true impact and value of initiative is measured in results. What good is much action if it amounts to little or nothing more than exercise in busyness?

Nothing even remotely close to this could be said about the twenty-sixth president of the United States. When Roosevelt employed his spirit of keen initiative, it was never random or without cause.

One of T.R.'s crowning achievements was the construction of the Panama Canal. Forty-eight miles wide, it connects the Atlantic Ocean to the Pacific Ocean via the Caribbean Sea. A French company had tried to build a canal through Panama in the late nineteenth century but met defeat, in part, with the malarial mosquitos that attacked most of the 22,000 laborers.

Therefore, after some wrangling, the United States decided to pursue the Panama Canal construction in 1902. But Roosevelt, his tenacious leadership notwithstanding, also experienced challenges and difficulties in completing the project, changing the management several times before he landed on a workable solution.

It was when he turned to the U.S. Army to finish the job that the best systems, processes, and command came together to get it done.

The work, indeed, was accomplished. Roosevelt knew and understood the value importance of this waterway and the benefit it would bring to the United States and his resolve would not allow such a vital effort to falter. Today, it stands as one of the most remarkable construction projects in the world and a testament to American ingenuity and trade.

Initiative makes history.

Roosevelt, like Churchill, was not the kind to let his life happen to him. He wrote his history, and in many ways, that of America in the process.

Time truly does not wait for anyone.
It will ignore and leave the passive behind.

Roosevelt, the Life

Many politicians are heavily criticized for their lack of true, clearly beneficial accomplishments. While this is not always valid, often it is.

Part of why there is ease in celebrating the career of Theodore Roosevelt is there was little he did that did not positively impact the American people, right a wrong, correct and injustice, or stand up for others.

Here are just a few:

★ He received the Nobel Peace Prize, and was the first statesman to do so, for his efforts to negotiate peace during the Russo-Japanese War.

★ He passed the Meat Inspection Act in 1904, in large part as a response to many of the work-related horrors exposed in Upton Sinclair's book, *The Jungle*.

★ His love for the outdoors prompted him to establish five national parks, fifty-one bird sanctuaries, four game reserves, and over 100 million acres of national forests. In addition, he created eighteen national monuments, including the Grand Canyon.

★ The strength and capability of the U.S. Navy was bolstered during T.R.'s presidency. Roosevelt believed in and loved the navy, having served as assistant secretary in a prior role.

★ He created the U.S. Forest Service, again reflecting his appreciation and dedication to the American outdoors and desire to protect her lands into perpetuity.

★ America even has the Teddy Bear because of Roosevelt as he was unwilling to shoot a bear that his hunting partners had tied to a tree. A local candy shop placed two bears in the window and asked permission to call them "Teddy" bears.* The rest is history.

Certainly, this is not an exhaustive list, but it demonstrates the power of Roosevelt's initiative as he proved to be, in multiple and impactful ways, such an enduring catalyst for America's distinctive national interests.

And all this from the youngest president to have ever served at forty-two years of age.

Roosevelt and the Presidency

The idea of the American president is a unique one. Not royalty, not a monarch, each action and venture is bound by constitutional constructs. Forty-six men have served this role. Perhaps few as boldly and tenaciously as Theodore Roosevelt.

Given that Roosevelt chose not to seek an additional term, which was his right, one can only imagine what other great feats and endeavors he could have achieved.

Even so, he remains one of the most remarkable and indelible of our presidents. There are others that deserve mention, but that's for another time. Another book, perhaps.

For now, history applauds an individual who overcame severe physical ailments as a child to rise to the presidency of the United States. TR's was a bold and tenacious leadership, much like the man himself. Though he would later regret it, the decision not to seek another term speaks to his character and commitment to democracy.

His life and leadership serve as a testament to the power of tenacity and resolve. His legacy is a powerful reminder to

---

* Morris, Edmund. *The Rise of Theodore Roosevelt* (New York: Random House, 1979), 432.

embrace initiative and the strenuous over that of ease and comfort.

The courage to face and overcome challenges is the mark that every leader desires to make on history. Roosevelt's spirit continues to inspire those who dare to step into the arena and change things for the better.

T.R.'s Leadership Principles

★ **Overcome Personal Challenges:** Roosevelt literally transformed himself from sickly to robust through sheer determination and consistent effort. Leaders must first master themselves before leading others.

★ **Embrace the Strenuous Life:** Roosevelt didn't just talk about hard work—he exemplified it. Leaders set the standard through action, not words, choosing the difficult path over the easy one.

★ **Take Bold Initiative:** Roosevelt seized opportunities to create positive change, whether as police commissioner, governor, or president. True leaders don't wait for permission to do what's right.

★ **Convict With Integrity:** Roosevelt fought corruption and championed justice regardless of political cost. His integrity wasn't situational—it was foundational to his leadership.

★ **Lead From the Front:** Whether charging up San Juan Hill or tackling domestic reforms, Roosevelt never asked others to take risks he wouldn't take himself. Real leadership is demonstrated, not delegated.

★ **Champion Bold Ideas:** Projects like the Panama Canal showcased Roosevelt's willingness to pursue ambitious goals despite obstacles. Leaders must think big and act decisively.

★ **Pursue Lifelong Learning:** Roosevelt's voracious reading and constant learning fueled his leadership. He proved that effective leaders never stop developing themselves.

Chapter Three

Henry Ford – American Industrialist

*"Industry is the soul of business and
the keystone of prosperity."*

—Charles Dickens

Henry Ford did not invent the automobile. Most credit either Gottlieb Daimler or Karl Benz, though there is evidence of a steam-engine vehicle built by Nicolas Joseph Cugnot of France in 1769.

What Ford did, due to his ground-breaking idea, was to make driving one more affordable for the general public as opposed to only the super wealthy. That vision, and supporting actions, providing the feeling and freedom of owning and operating the American automobile, is why Ford is so revered in this arena.

No, Ford did not create the automobile, but he would go on to help millions who would have otherwise never received the chance to discover the joy of owning what was once considered a luxury.

The impact of Ford's vision is also quantified in remarkable statistics. In 1908, there was roughly one car for every 85 Americans. By 1927, after nearly two decades of Model T production, this had changed to one car for every 5.3 Americans, demonstrating how Ford's mission to democratize the automobile had fundamentally transformed American society.*

It should also be noted that just because what some called "driverless carriages" had already been developed, that doesn't necessarily equal that Ford couldn't have been the one to have done so.

He certainly had the acumen and capacity.

Ford was always fascinated by gears and machinery. At age thirteen, his father gave him a pocket watch, which he promptly proceeded to strip and then reassemble. Once family and friends learned he had that knack and ability, he was asked to repair their timepieces as well.

Though raised doing farmwork, he found the work itself unsatisfying and left it behind to become an apprentice at a shipyard as, what else, a machinist. In 1887 he built his first engine, a quad-cylinder, after repairing an Otto engine. He would later go on to build a two-cylinder as well in 1890.

His first motor vehicle was built in 1896, powered by a two-cylinder engine. It was rudimentary, but perhaps not for the time. Affectionally dubbed the Quadricycle, it had four horsepower at 400 rpm but could achieve up to 8 horsepower at its maximum speed. This early model also included twenty-eight-inch bicycle tires and a three-quart gas tank. The Quadricycle had a 2-speed planetary transmission with no reverse gear. The belt drive system used leather belts that could be shifted between two sets of pulleys.

---

* Brinkley, Douglas, *Wheels for the World: Henry Ford, His Company, and a Century of Progress* (Viking Press, 2003), 278.

Ford would go on to drive it approximately 1,000 miles before beginning work on his second vehicle in 1896. All this transpired while Ford was working as an engineer with the Edison Illuminating Company of Detroit.

Ford's love for the vehicle would follow him and lead to redesigns and valuable connections with the likes of Thomas Edison and William Murphy, a lumber magnate who would be instrumental in helping him fund the start of the Detroit Automobile Company.

It's unlikely that most would remember that company as it suffered a demise due to internal issues such as Ford focusing on racing car development instead of production vehicles. Only about twenty were produced and were expensive ($1,000-$1,200). They were also unreliable even though Ford's perfectionism constantly delayed production.

The Start of Something Big

It is typically recommended that entrepreneurs and startups not name their companies or businesses after themselves. Perhaps because it could be seen as vain or self-indulgent. After all, the best leaders have their focus squarely on how their organization and mission can impact and raise the life of others, not their own legacies.

History says the founder of Ford Motor Company was able to balance both realities.

It's also plausible that ego never entered the mind of Henry Ford as he envisioned and subsequently launched what would, one day, become an automobile juggernaut with annual revenue of over 170 billion dollars. This was not the only company to bear his name, the first being the Henry Ford Company in 1901, from which he would leave two years later.

Ford is not the only successful business with the name of the person who created it.

That list is almost endless, including widely known companies like J.P. Morgan, Carnegie Steel, J.C. Penney, Levi Strauss, Mars, Sears, and, of course, HERSHEY, which even has the name larger and in gold letters.

But like Ford, Hershey would be remembered for much more than the transformative products he would make and sell. It is the impact on the greater good that motivated these individuals beyond simply a bottom line.

Vision and What Ought to Be

If the overemphasis on profit, mainly from his investors, doomed the Detroit Motor Company, the vision Henry Ford had in his mind to provide an affordable vehicle for the common man would prove to be a catalyst for the success of this new venture, which was basically a reorganization of the last.

Vision is not only what can be, but what, in the mind of the dreamer, ought to be. Henry Ford could be considered and remembered as the "people's" entrepreneur. While it is always a business's primary intent to stay financially solvent, that can't be the only objective.

At least, it shouldn't be.

History remembers those who give, not take. Ego and self-indulgence are not quality characteristics for leaders of any stripe, not the least of which those who would be in business.

It seems Henry Ford instinctively knew this and, while he was certainly interested in profiting from his ideas, had in his mind his dream of helping ordinary people achieve *their* dream of owning a motorized automobile.

Thus, the name Ford has a different ring to it when heard throughout the annals of time as opposed to a Jay Gould or even Ken Lay (Enron).

A vision can be simple but still go deep.

For a vision to resonate, live, and flourish, there must be enough solid ground in which it can take root and thrive.

Vision is not only what can be, but what,
in the mind of the dreamer, ought to be.

The Catalyst

The first modern automobile is considered to be the Benz Motorcar, built by Carl Benz in 1885.

While it would be tempting to say it looks akin to an elaborate tricycle and could only seat two to three people, it proved the concept of gas-powered vehicles and would help spark the beginnings of a vehicular revolution.

The first American-made gasoline car was sold in 1898 at an exorbitant amount of $1,000, approximately $36,000 in today's money. Overall, prices for vehicles in the early 1900s ranged from $1,000 to $3,000, depending on the model and type.

Clearly horses were cheaper.

The leap from a dependable, less expensive animal to a new, relatively untested machine was one that many were unwilling, if not unable, to make.

Again, every dream, every vision, and every idea needs a catalyst. Henry Ford desired that his countrymen not be prohibited from sharing in what was, at the time, a world-changing innovation simply because it was deemed an unaffordable amenity.

Ford was too much of a pragmatist, not to mention a true patriot, to let that stand.

The People's Entrepreneur

"A business that makes nothing but money is a poor business." Henry Ford

While he didn't invent the automobile, what he was able to do with the creation of the modern vehicle is no less impressive, especially given both the goal and the results.

The reality of value is woven into every enterprise and leadership opportunity. Businesses hire individuals because they believe they will bring value to the success of the organization and, in return, receive an exchange of value in a salary and benefits, not to mention that of being a part of a successful and reputable company.

However, should that be where the value stops? Pioneers like Ford are remembered as those who helped fuel the American spirit because what his vision, designs, and innovation brought to his compatriots, and even the world, transcends merely employing and compensating a workforce.

It can't be stated enough that the fruit of all that Henry Ford accomplished for American enterprise and the future of the U.S. auto industry began with a dream and a vision. But ideas don't work unless people do, and they are validated by outcomes.

Ford left such an indelible mark on history because his achievements matched his vision. They were large in both scope and depth.

Exactly how did Henry Ford add so much to the progress of American society in the world of industry and manufacturing?

That's the power of vision.

Every dream, every vision,
and every idea needs a catalyst.

The Beloved Model T

Before its launch in 1908, there were nineteen prototypes developed for what would become one of Ford's favorite designs. It was named "T" for the twentieth letter in the alphabet given this was the product that finally met success. Ford and his team developed several experimental models, working through the alphabet from Model A to Model S.*

The Model T represented the culmination of these efforts, though its designation as "T" was simply the next letter in Ford's alphabetical naming sequence rather than any special significance of being the twentieth attempt.**

---

* Casey, Robert, *The Model T: A Centennial History* (Johns Hopkins University Press, 2008), 28.

** Brinkley, Douglas, *Wheels for the World: Henry Ford, His Company, and a Century of Progress* (Viking Press, 2003), 112.

Given the aforementioned expense of the average vehicle at the time, the introduction of something new, and, at $850 for the touring edition, at least a little more affordable, helped make this first product commercially sold quite popular.

Ford's true innovation in affordability would come through his mastery of mass production techniques. Through continuous refinement of the assembly line process and economies of scale, Ford achieved dramatic price reductions over the following years. The touring car price dropped to $690 by 1911, then to $490 by 1915, and finally reached its lowest point of $290 in 1924.*

These price reductions, combined with the car's durability and ease of maintenance, transformed the Model T from merely another automobile on the market into a vehicle that truly put America on wheels.

---

* Sorensen, Charles E., *My Forty Years with Ford* (Norton, 1956), 137-139.

This yielded another bit of fruit for those deciding about, and often wrestling with, the idea of progressing beyond the horse and carriage towards wheels and an engine.

It seems Ford was thinking of types of drivers as well. In its design, there was left-side steering and sufficient ground clearance for those who would be driving in rural areas. The Model T was also the first vehicle to have all its parts made by one company. It was truly a Ford product, built for the American public and marketed as such.

In Ford's own words he was recorded to say, "*I will build a motor car for the great multitude. It will be large enough for the family, but small enough for the individual to run and care for.*"[**] This was validated by the fact that Ford would go on to sell 15,007,034 Model Ts between 1908 to 1927.[***]

[**] Ford, Henry, *My Life and Work: An Autobiography of Henry Ford* (Garden City Publishing, 1922), 73.

[***] Collier, Peter and Horowitz, David, *The Fords: An American Epic* (Summit Books, 1987), 89. The exact final production number of 15,007,034 units is also documented in Ford Motor Company archives.

Would the eventual evolution of American transportation have been much slower and more gradual had not Ford produced a less expensive automobile like the Model T?

Arguably, yes.

One Thing Leads to Another: The Assembly Line

Another Ford-exclusive contribution to the growth of American industry in the early 1900s was the innovation of the assembly line. The concept of this type of manufacturing process was not new and could be found in meatpacking plants and textile mills.

Yet Ford is credited with innovating this system by pioneering a *moving* production line, with the key feature being the conveyor belt. While this type of machinery was used in slaughterhouses, Ford brought it into the automobile manufacturing space, allowing workers to be stationary while building each vehicle.

This reduced the time required to assemble a unit from twelve hours down to an hour and thirty-three minutes. That's beyond innovative. That's groundbreaking.

It fostered the idea of specialized workers for each part of the process. As with many of Ford's ideas and advancements, the reimagining of the assembly line went beyond the function itself.

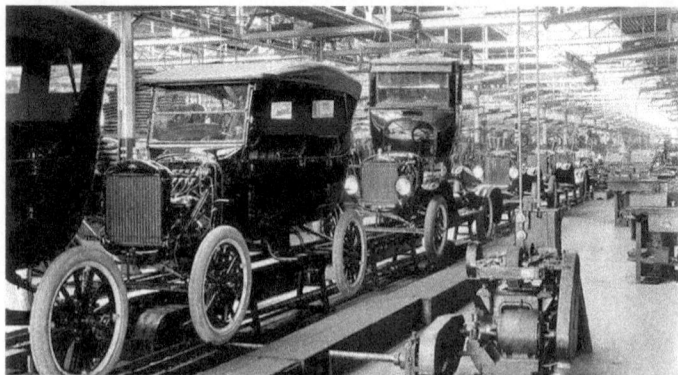

Given that workers could be stationary, this led to the idea of specialists and dedicated craftsmen for a particular position, though the tasks could become mundane and monotonous at times. It also reduced more than the time it took to produce a vehicle.

The introduction of the moving assembly line in 1913 reduced the Model T's chassis assembly time from 12.5 hours to 93 minutes, while simultaneously improving quality and reducing worker injuries.*

As mentioned, it continued to decrease the price as well, again increasing the purchase power for more Americans. Ford's implementation of the assembly line wasn't merely a technological innovation—it was a social revolution that transformed the relationship between workers, their work, and the final product.**

Success Creates Opportunity

Businesses drive economic growth. Capitalism is not a bad word. A thriving company that pursues both profits and the good of their people is one worth remembering. Ford's innovation not only impacted the manufacturing of vehicles, but those doing the work, not to mention their families and economic community.

While unemployment was low, at around 3%, working hours were long, often fifty-four to sixty-three per week, and accidents were common. The expansion of automobile manufacturing had a ripple effect on supply chains that extended to those who manufactured parts and material such as steel, rubber, glass, and the like.

---

* Nevins, Allan, *Ford: The Times, The Man, The Company* (Charles Scribner's Sons, 1954).
** Snow, Richard, *I Invented the Modern Age: The Rise of Henry Ford* (Scribner, 2013).

But it could be argued that the biggest impact was on the Ford employee himself. A $5 wage for a day's work was implemented, which was much higher compared to the going rate at the time.

Clearly this improved the lives of the workforce but had yet another positive effect. It would go on to set a precedent for fair labor practices and guard against a disparity between the work being done and appropriate compensation.

Ford also advocated for a five-day, forty-hour workweek. In an era where work-life balance was unheard of, he opened the door for his employees to enjoy more leisure time and a healthier employment experience.

Ford's Leadership Legacy

Perhaps Henry Ford's driving force (no pun intended) was simply to produce a low-cost vehicle so more of his fellow Americans could own one.

Mr. Ford's contribution to our civilization extends far beyond his industrial accomplishments. His philosophy that high wages and reasonable hours make for both prosperity and contentment, his demonstration that a useful commodity may be made so cheap that it becomes available to the whole population, made him one of the foremost leaders in social progress.*

The leadership Ford displayed in growing the Ford Motor Company, can't be discounted. And while no CEO or business owner is perfect, there are several reasons Henry Ford gets a chapter in this book.

What are the essential leadership lessons the life of Henry Ford left behind? What fitting example did he set?

---

* Rae, John B., *The American Automobile Industry* (Twayne Publishers, 1984), 45.

The Power of Visionary Action

It all starts with vision.

What if Henry Ford never had the idea of designing and building a vehicle that would be more affordable than what the market offered at the time? Would someone have taken up that challenge at some point?

Perhaps.

But Ford didn't wait. The vision of making this relatively new product more accessible drove his choices and pivotal actions to advance that dream.

Action separates the dreamers from the doers. Many people have ambitious thoughts that populate the mind and may even make it to paper or a rough plan. A vision worth having is one worth pursuing.

It eventually becomes visible and tangible. John Maxwell states, *"Lots of people have good ideas in the shower. What matters is what you do once you dry off."*

And in Ford's own words, *"You can't build a reputation on what you are going to do."*

Ford is a shining example that thousands and thousands of doors that lead to opportunity can be opened by not only possessing a vivid vision but being possessed by the same.

Imagine what was going through his mind upon seeing his creation rolling off the assembly line or being driven proudly on the streets of Detroit and beyond.

Was it as he pictured? Was it everything he imagined? Chances are it came very close.

Very close indeed.

While no pursuit of a dream is perfect, and can be ladened with pitfalls and setbacks, it must be compelling enough to persevere to see its fruition.

But it all starts with that snapshot of a preferable future. It all starts with *vision*.

> *A vision worth having is one worth pursuing.*
> *It eventually becomes visible and tangible.*

The Ford Family of Employees

What makes a great employee? What gets people excited about leaving a warm bed and driving (if not working remotely) to a place, perhaps not even close to their home, to trade their time and effort for a paycheck?

Is there something that separates the U.S. workforce, or at least differentiates them in a way that reflects American values and ideals? Is that even a genuine consideration or thought?

While arguments abound as to the actual reason for the increase in pay, which included salary and bonus, the reality is that Ford did so, in part, to decrease turnover and maintain a healthy workforce.

On January 5, 1914, Henry Ford stunned the industrial world by announcing that Ford Motor Company would pay qualified workers a minimum wage of $5 per day, more than doubling the average autoworker's wage of $2.34 per day. The program also reduced the workday from nine to eight hours.*

This had a tremendous effect on the corporate culture and productivity of the organization. Employee turnover dropped from 370% to 16% within two years, absentees fell, and daily production reached 4,000 cars.

---

* Watts, Steven, *The People's Tycoon: Henry Ford and the American Century* (Vintage Books, 2006), 178-179.

There were conditions to this new wage and set of benefits and the accountability practices that were employed would be considered invasive by today's standards.

However, at the heart of the increase was Ford's paternal instincts in doing the best he could to care for his workers, at the same time bolstering output.

Pioneering Industrialist

Henry Ford should be remembered as more than just a successful entrepreneur and innovator. He certainly was that, but he was also something more.

His belief in the automobile and desire for any of his fellow citizens to be able to own one separates him from the business owner who places profit above people. Or purpose.

His vision and mission took the Ford Motor Company beyond the nuts and bolts of the assembly line and helped to shift the entire landscape of industrial American society.

By providing a fair wage and better working conditions, he sought to treat his workers with fairness and respect as an attempt to create a corporate culture of opportunity.

While his record is not as pristine as other patriots, especially with rumors of antisemitism, his example of transformative and visionary leadership is secure.

He will forever be remembered as the people's tycoon and a shining example of the impact purpose over profit can have on the world.

Ford's Leadership Principles

★ **Ground Vision in Purpose:** Ford's dream wasn't just about profit—it was about making automobiles accessible to everyday Americans. True vision serves others while building success.

★ **Perfect Through Prototypes:** Ford's relentless refinement from Model A through T shows that greatness comes through continuous improvement, not instant perfection.

★ **Transform Through Innovation:** Ford didn't just build cars—he revolutionized how they were made. Leaders must be willing to completely reimagine how things are done.

★ **Value Your People:** Ford's $5 workday wasn't just generosity—it was revolutionary thinking about the relationship between company and worker. Leaders understand that taking care of people powers progress.

★ **Balance Profit and Purpose:** Ford proved that social good and business success aren't mutually exclusive. Leaders can pursue profit while positively impacting society.

★ **Master Your Craft Early:** Ford's early fascination with mechanics shaped his future. Great leaders often build on foundational passions and skills developed in youth.

★ **Challenge Current Constraints:** Ford wasn't satisfied with cars being only for the wealthy. Real leaders don't accept artificial limitations. They find ways to break them.

Chapter Four

George Patton – American General

"May God have mercy for my
enemies because I won't."

—George S. Patton

War is hell.

This is not a literal statement, but a widely felt sentiment expressed by those who've had to fight, regardless the conflict or scale.

While nations raging against others has been an age-old reality for almost all of man's existence, it is warriors, and those who can lead them successfully on the chosen battlefields, become noteworthy if they are able to lead their armies to victory rather than taste bitter defeat.

Few embodied that idea of the former as did America's General George Patton.

While there are more, and some his contemporaries, the combination of his raw, no-nonsense, not to mention gutsy, military acumen and tenacity place him above many in the chronicles of American's wartime history.*

An Unwelcomed War

Much like with the first World War, many were believing, and hoping, that the United States would not enter what was emerging as another global conflict that began in 1939.

The concept and practice of isolationism drove that idea, as well as the assertion by Congress and President Franklin D. Roosevelt that the ideological and practical catalyst, and what might result, did not genuinely interest the US.

The memory of World War I's senseless carnage, the failure of Wilson's crusade to make the world safe for democracy, and the cynical manipulation of American idealism by the Allies to secure American entry into the war in 1917 had created a powerful anti-interventionist sentiment in American society.**

Further, America had more than enough with which to contend, not the least being the Great Depression. Therefore, those living in the United States generally felt "safe" from European wars and either detached or indifferent to what Hitler was attempting to do.

Of course, all that changed on December 7th, 1941.

The surprise and brutal attack on Pearl Harbor, much like Germany's submarine warfare during the first World War, left a president, his cabinet, and congressional leaders in the U.S. little choice other than to retaliate and engage with enemies they would have rather left alone. World War II would eventually involve almost *every* part of the world.

---

* Bradley, Omar N., *A Soldier's Story* (Henry Holt and Company, 1951), 182-183.

** Jonas, Manfred, *Isolationism in America, 1935-1941* (Cornell University Press, 1966), 35.

France, Great Britain, the United States, and the Soviet Union composed the Allies, while Germany, Italy, and Japan were named the Axis powers.

World War II was a massive and bloody conflict. It would cost a total of between 40,000,000 and 50,000,000 lives.***

War Demands Warriors

Any crusade calls for those willing to do whatever it takes to win and defeat the enemy, or enemies. That's not a revolutionary statement. It's not even very profound.

However, the scale and weight of a truth can be impacted by that of the situation to which it's applied. This kind of war needed a warrior *not* like others. One like George Patton.

To illustrate, perhaps some of the general's own words (some which have been slightly edited for language) can serve to illustrate the value and strength he brought to the forces of good during WWII.

From "The Armies of George Patton" (George Forty),

> *"Men, this stuff that some sources sling around about America wanting out of this war, not wanting to fight, is a crock of bull——.*

***

*** www.brittanica.com

Americans love to fight, traditionally. All real Americans love the sting and clash of battle.

You are here today for three reasons. First, because you are here to defend your homes and your loved ones. Second, you are here for your own self-respect because you would not want to be anywhere else. Third, you are here because you are real men, and all real men like to fight. When you, here, every one of you, were kids, you all admired the champion marble player, the fastest runner, the toughest boxer, the big-league ball players, and the All-American football players. Americans love a winner. Americans will not tolerate a loser. Americans despise cowards. Americans play to win all of the time. I wouldn't give a hoot in hell for a man who lost and laughed. That's why Americans have never lost nor will ever lose a war; for the very idea of losing is hateful to an American.

You are not all going to die. Only two percent of you right here today would die in a major battle. Death must not be feared. Death, in time, comes to all men. Yes, every man is scared in his first battle. If he says he's not, he's a liar. Some men are cowards, but they fight the same as the brave men or they get the hell slammed out of them watching men fight who are just as scared as they are. The real hero is the man who fights even though he is scared. Some men get over their fright in a minute under fire. For some, it takes an hour. For some, it takes days. But a real man will never let his fear of death overpower his honor, his sense of duty to his country, and his innate manhood."

One can hear the pride and respect the general had for his men, the magnitude of the moment, as well as the horror of war in every word of this speech.

Even still, Patton inspired more than confidence in his men to triumph in battle. He tied it to the American ideal and the why behind the will to win.

War demands warriors.

George Patton not only fervently believed in his country, he lived with an undying passion for the military sworn to protect her. That began in his youth, perhaps spurred by the fact that his ancestors fought in the American Revolution and the Civil War. This likely brought about a desire to carve a path of military realization for himself.

Patton's childhood home in San Gabriel was filled with military memorabilia, including his grandfather's Confederate sword and photographs of relatives in uniform. This martial atmosphere, combined with his father's extensive library of military histories, created an environment where young George's future seemed almost predestined.*

That journey began in 1904 with his acceptance to the Virginia Military Institute before moving on to West Point a year later.

Grace and Accidents

It might be hard to imagine General Geroge Patton as anything but the hardtack commanding officer who would earn the name "Old Blood and Guts" during his boisterous military career. It could be just as difficult to attach a word like grace or poise to one whose language and leadership style might be considered anything but elegant.

However, one of the lesser-known chapters of Patton's life involved his artful skill with a sword.

General Patton, in his youth, was an excellent and skilled swordsman. His father purchased a used bayonet for young Patton, and he practiced on a cactus with less than stellar results. He was also hopelessly accident prone, even suffering a

---

* Hirshson, Stanley P., *General Patton: A Soldier's Life* (Harper Collins, 2002), 33.

skull fracture that may have led to a life of violent and profane language.

These, perhaps, may not be considered the best of combinations, but it could be said that Patton was a mixed bag of strengths and weaknesses, much like anyone would be.

Regarding the sword, it is an object that would follow him throughout his career, and before, including entering the Olympics, and more than just in fencing. Patton competed in the 1912 Stockholm Olympics in the Modern Pentathlon, placing fifth overall despite a disappointing shooting round. The experience would later influence his emphasis on physical fitness and competitive spirit in military training.*

A New and Distinctive Saber for the U.S. Cavalry

While reportedly never officially used in battle, the *Model 1913 Cavalry Saber* is a piece of American military history that can tell one a much about the kind of stuff that made George Patton one of her greatest warriors.

For the American soldier, the use of swords in battle dates to the Revolutionary War and those serving under George Washington. This regal piece of military equipment was not just for fighting, but represented bravery, leadership, and even self-sacrifice.

---

* D'Este, Carlo, *Patton: A Genius for War* (Harper Collins, 1995), 89-93.

No doubt Patton knew this when he designed this particular model.

The Patton Saber was the last warfare sword designed for the U.S. military, marking the end of this era in warfare. While it never saw combat, its development reflected Patton's deep understanding of cavalry tactics and his ability to blend traditional military values with modern combat requirements.**

How important is the manner and particulars of how a sword is engineered? In the heat of battle, clearly, one only needs it to accomplish its primary purpose, neutralizing the enemy. A deeper look, however, can shed light on why this weapon was unique to this American general, so much so that it would become known as "the Patton Sword."

★ **The blade**: A departure from the standard curved design, the Model 1913 featured one that was straight and double edged, intended to thrust, instead of slashing, which improved its effectiveness during a cavalry charge.

★ **Balance**: Length and weight of any sword is of significance. This model was roughly thirty-five inches and two and half pounds, which increased its reach and maneuverability.

★ **Grip**: Made of wood and covered in leather, it was wrapped in wire to ensure more durability as well as comfort.

★ **Scabbard**: Fashioned from steel and more than ample protection for the blade. Strategically designed to be worn on the left side, allowing it to be drawn quickly with the right hand.

★ **Overall Design**: The blueprint was inspired by the European cavalry's methods and his opinion that

---

** Meilinger, Phillip S., *American Military Culture and Strategy* (Military Review, 2007), 74-76.

thrusting was more effective than cutting as it relates to horse-ridden combat.

The Patton Saber represented more than just a weapon—it symbolized the modernization of American cavalry and Patton's innovative approach to warfare. Although it arrived at the sunset of cavalry combat, its development demonstrated the American military's ability to blend traditional martial values with modern tactical requirements.*

Clearly this was no ordinary blade. It was marked and defined by its creator and represented much about the American warrior spirit.

Words That Cut Deep

Returning to Patton's words from earlier in the chapter, one does not need to read between the lines to understand and embrace the meaning behind each one. But perhaps a careful dissection and analysis of selected key phrases, coupled with associated events from his life, could adequately show the heart and soul of one of America's most famous, perhaps even infamous, war heroes.

Words certainly do matter. As mentioned in Chapter 1, for any leader, or even the average communicator, substance carries weight depending on the ability and artfulness of the speaker.

Patton was in a category all his own when it came to style and delivery. One can only imagine that all that he conveyed, whether on the battlefield or in his talks, was colored and infused by a passion and zeal for total victory.

If nothing else, Patton led with an honest perspective as it related to war, fighting, and how to best engage in the defense of liberty and freedom.

---

* Phillips, Gervase, "The Saber During the American Civil War and After," *American Military History Journal*, Vol. 62, No. 1 (2001), 81-82.

Americans Love to Fight

Seemingly a contrarian statement, as it includes the word *love*. People love their spouses, children, some love their possessions, and others certain foods or travel destinations.

But love to fight? Fighting is violence. It involves pain and often death.

Certainly, there are more layers to this statement. It would be easy to suppose that Patton drew from not only his own experiences in making this claim, but also from the gutsy history of a nation that dared to wage war against a superior enemy to gain its independence.

The love of an ideal will inspire a love to fight when called. Fighting just for its own sake is senseless, perhaps even sadistic. But battling for a belief as valuable as liberty is more than just and pure.

George Patton proved that, not just in America's second global conflict, but throughout his entire military career, as an early account demonstrates.

The love of an ideal will inspire
a love to fight when called.

Border Patrol

One incident that would help shape Patton's reputation for boldness occurred during the 1916 Mexican Punitive Expedition. As military historian John S.D. Eisenhower recounts, this campaign marked one of Patton's first opportunities to demonstrate his aggressive leadership style in actual combat conditions.**

** Eisenhower, John S.D. *Intervention!: The United States and the Mexican Revolution, 1913-1917* (W.W. Norton, 1993), 217.

Around October 1915, Venustiano Carranza became the head of the Mexican Government, angering Fransico "Pancho" Villa, who was his political rival.

Villa retaliated by attacking U.S. nationals in northern Mexico and destroying their property.

President Woodrow Willson would respond by ordering military action against Villa, placing General John Pershing in command and given the objective of putting an end to the raids and capturing Pancho.

Wilson stated:

"An adequate force will be sent at once in pursuit of Villa with the single object of capturing him and putting a stop to his forays. This can and will be done in entirely friendly aid to the constituted authorities in Mexico and with scrupulous respect for the sovereignty of that Republic."

While this kind of military operation might be considered somewhat standard, the story of Patton and a chance encounter on border patrol and a supply run was anything but. It would also be a foretelling of the kind of battlefield leader that was emerging.

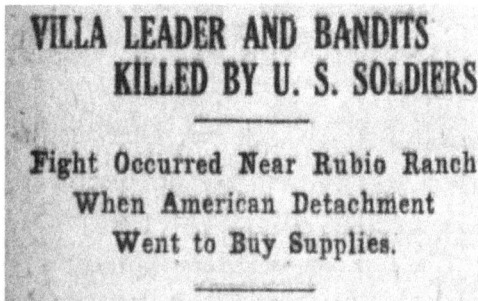

VILLA LEADER AND BANDITS KILLED BY U. S. SOLDIERS

Fight Occurred Near Rubio Ranch When American Detachment Went to Buy Supplies.

While leading an expedition to buy food for U.S. soldiers, one of the interpreters recognized someone at one of the stops. Being a former bandit himself helped with the recall. Patton seized on this chance intel, knowing that one of the leaders of Villa's gang was reported to live nearby, and began a search of farms in the area.

The May 1916 encounter at San Miguelito ranch proved to be one of Patton's first tests of combat leadership. As military historian Martin Blumenson documents:

When Patton and his small patrol approached the ranch house, three Mexican riders suddenly burst from the building. Patton, positioned at the front of the house, fired with his Colt pistol, killing two of the bandits' horses. In the ensuing chaos, the third rider escaped. Upon spotting a larger group of mounted men approaching, Patton made the tactical decision to withdraw. He ordered the dead bandits secured to their vehicles before making a successful retreat to the American lines.*

Leadership is action. Leadership is not a title or position, or even tied to a particular task, except for the execution of it. That should include frequently taking calculated risks and not settling for the normal or even the expected, a trait that would follow Patton throughout his career.

He seemed to relish both engaging and taking the fight to the enemy, versus the other way around.

The skirmish at San Miguelito marked Patton's first experience with combat leadership and his first time killing in battle. The incident made a lasting impression on General Pershing, who mentioned it specifically in his reports and later cited it as evidence of Patton's natural aptitude for command under fire.**

---

* Blumenson, Martin, *The Patton Papers: 1885-1940* (Houghton Mifflin, 1972), 231-232.

** Pershing, John J, *My Experiences in the World War.* Vol. 1. (Frederick A. Stokes, 1931).

You Are Here for Three Reasons

Given the kind of loss that is experienced in any war, and tremendous price that is paid, the justification must be its equal. The pacifist would never be convinced of any rationalization for the killing and destruction that these kinds of hostilities rend to nations and, ultimately, the world.

George Patton was certainly no pacifist. But neither was he a fiend or lunatic.

War, for the sake of, is madness or the result of an unhinged ego and the delusions of any would-be conqueror. While history has plenty of these demagoguery types scattered throughout the vast array of people groups, there have been yet others that chose to fight with the proper motive, with honor and gravity.

War Needs a Reason

Wars are started, joined, and ended. Hopefully sooner rather than later, as to avoid as much death as possible. Knowing, and carrying, the cause of either affecting or suffering that ultimate cost could be essential to exact all that's necessary to prove victorious on any given battlefield.

Not all campaigns are just. Not all motives are pure. The balance of any great leader's influence will be impacted by the integrity of his actions.

War is bad enough. Pursuit of ill-gotten gains deepens the misery.

In his speech, Patton reminded his men of three noble reasons for not only their existence, but the role they would play in the upcoming engagement. The fact that the general delivered all of his remarks without notes is further evidence of the conviction and resolve behind this hopeful message.

As mentioned, George Patton came from a military lineage. No doubt stories were passed on and a personal history that formed the brave spirit he would carry and be able to share.

That's a bit of the kind of legacy any great leader can extend.

You Are Here to Defend Your Homes and Your Loved Ones

Could there be any greater motive than this? Of all that can be destroyed by war, human lives, and where they dwell, are the most treasured. Buildings and weaponry can be replaced. Even soldiers understand their safety is certainly not guaranteed, and, while any loss of life is devastating, the innocents in harm's way are an exception to the rest.

It's clear this is what General Patton was seeking to convey: the high value of people, especially those these soldiers loved dear. The sanctity of life is not necessarily an American ideal, but in this speech, it certainly was an overarching theme.

One can only imagine the thoughts and images soldiers carried with them that were as real as the oft-tattered photographs they kept close to their hearts. Heroically they would wrestle the will to win along with the thought or dread that they might never return home to their wives and children.

Patton understood this and used his words not only to inspire but also to honor their beloved families.

Incidentally, the casualty rate under his leadership was relatively low compared to other commands. Despite his aggressive tactics, he understood that speed and decisive action often saved more lives than cautious advances.*

---

* Atkinson, Rick. *The Day of Battle: The War in Sicily and Italy, 1943-1944* (Henry Holt, 2007), 312.

You Are Here for Your Own Self-Respect

Respect can be a buzzword or fuzzy term in many circles. Not so in the army. And not so for George Patton. For the general, respect was an essential principle and core value for his and anyone's leadership, regardless of arena.

Clearly military discipline is linked to respect. For those in command, but also for self.

Patton believed in this connection as a key to building a cohesive, effective unit. Also, self-respect is an essential element of morale. Patton respected his troops. They, in turn, respected him and themselves. This boosted morale, which lifts all.

Every human being desires and deserves to be treated with a certain level of human pride and dignity, including how they view themselves. The general's own writings reflect this belief. In his personal papers, he wrote, *"A man of great self-respect is likely to be a good soldier... Wars are not won by men who have no pride in being soldiers."**

Patton was able to tap into this and preserve it in the face of the worst that war had to offer. He believed that maintaining self-respect and showing respect to others harnessed this sense of worth and dignity and could insulate from the harsh conditions of war.

You Are Real Men

Masculinity is not a bad word. At least, not always.

Consider the era.

This was 1940s America. "Real men" was neither confusing nor insulting. It was a direct appeal to their sense of manhood and bravery. Principal qualities and characteristics necessary for the bloody task at hand. Further, labeling all as such

---

* Province, Charles M. *The Unknown Patton* (Hippocrene Books, 1983), 87.

reinforced the idea of a brotherhood and a select group of warriors.

All this was normal, especially in military culture.

Americans Love a Winner

Is this philosophy? Is it an attitude? Motivational happy talk?

No. This statement was neither vacuous nor ramble. Consider the brief life and history of America up to that point. While there were incredible losses, victory was a part of the national DNA.

Patton believed in that indominable spirit, as well as pride in a country that achieved independence, survived a war against itself, and survived other conflicts, not the least of which was another world war a couple of decades before.

He was challenging them to become a part of another season of triumph.

You Are Not All Going to Die

405,399 American soldiers lost their lives in the second World War. How would one know if he would be counted in that kind of dreadful number?

The answer, of course, is he wouldn't. This, no doubt, would have preyed on the emotional as well as psychological awareness of every troop.

Patton knew this was one of the most common fears of every soldier and addressed it head on, even providing statistics that he hoped to be reassuring. Doom and dread can creep into any fight or battle, literal or figurative. The general wanted to dispel the notion that every soldier was doomed from the start.

Ideally, this would serve as some reassurance and lessen anxiety, as much as could be achieved in the face of such an ebon prospect. Patton had no problem confronting these kinds of stark realities directly and honestly.

It was the mission on which he wanted his army to focus. And to know why it was worth winning. They would be the instruments of a righteous conquest.

And the general would lead them. A general who was the right leader for his times.

Leadership is not a title or position,
or even tied to a particular task, except for the execution of it.

Legacy

George Patton's leadership and impact has far outlived the battlefields of the Second World War. It is a true testament to the strength and resolution of gutsy leadership. His combination of discipline, respect, willpower, and his care for his troops not only endeared him to them, but left a permanent mark on American miliary history.

Roger Nye, in his study of Patton's leadership style, notes that Patton's concept of leadership was inseparable from action. He believed that soldiers would follow a leader who demonstrated personal courage and decisive action rather than one who simply issued orders.*

---

* Nye, Roger H. *The Patton Mind: The Professional Development of an Extraordinary Leader* (Avery Publishing Group, 1993),.45.

While his objective, win at all costs, was always clear, his leadership style was deep and often complex. This served him well when America needed it most.

His death on December 21st, 1945, did not equal the kind of bold and daring life he led. However, his story and influence reverberate throughout time as reminders of strategic and audacious leadership. He was able to inspire with both words *and* actions.

Bold, innovative, and often irreverent, he stands as a key figure in America's fight to preserve freedom.

George Patton demonstrated, always, the will to protect the country he dutifully served.

He and his beloved troops.

Patton's Leadership Principles

★ **Cultivate Unwavering Conviction:** Patton's absolute belief in victory infected his entire command. He showed how a leader's confidence shapes their organization's spirit.

★ **Balance Tradition and Innovation:** The "Patton Sword" exemplified his ability to honor military tradition while embracing new tactics. Leaders must bridge the old and new.

★ **Demand Excellence Relentlessly:** Patton accepted nothing less than the highest standards from himself and his troops. His example proves that expectations drive performance.

★ **Calculate Bold Risks:** While known for aggression, Patton's attacks were carefully planned. True leaders balance audacity with careful preparation.

★ **Connect Purpose to Action:** Patton tied every mission to larger meaning, showing that troops fight harder when they understand the "why" behind orders.

★ **Face Hard Truths:** Whether discussing casualties or fear, Patton was brutally honest about war's realities. Leaders must confront difficult facts directly.

★ **Project Strength While Showing Heart:** Behind Patton's tough exterior was genuine care for his men. Leaders can be both demanding and deeply concerned for their people.

Chapter Five

John Wayne – American Actor

"It's kind of a sad thing when a normal love of country makes you a super patriot. I do think we have a pretty wonderful country, and I thank God that He chose me to live here."

—John Wayne

The American Western. No other country has anything like it. Maybe because there's so much of America *in* them. With a panoramic view of the Montana or Texas skyline, sprawling sagas of frontier life would unfold in exciting and dramatic fashion given the right script and lead actor.

Few actors, if any, fit this mold like the man who would become known and remembered as "The Duke."

Standing right at six foot, four inches, and weighing 240 lbs., he more than fit the bill for any tough and rugged character in films like *The Searchers, Rio Bravo, Stagecoach, Fort Apache, Red River, True Grit,* and many more.

In fact, John Wayne would go on to appear in 169 films, and a total of 179 productions overall, with his last being

The Shootist, a film about a sheriff turned gunfighter dying of cancer.

In real life, Wayne would face a similar scenario.

While all his films were not Westerns, it would be hard not to argue that it is *the* genre for which he is best known. Those who followed his movies can picture the stride, the taut facial expression, and, of course, the unique voice inflection that would become synonymous with one of the most iconic actors of his era, if not of all time.

John Wayne, through his portrayals, and real-life ideals, would personify and promote what it meant to be a true American and what he considered the ideal man.

Cultural historian Garry Wills argues that John Wayne became more than just an actor; he emerged as a symbol of American values and leadership that transcended his film roles, shaping the nation's understanding of moral courage and decisive action.*

Neither John nor Wayne were his given names. He was born Marion Robert Morrison. That certainly doesn't have the

---

* Wills, Garry, *John Wayne's America: The Politics of Celebrity* (Simon & Schuster, 1997).

same kind of ring as the name that would become inextricably linked to Western folklore in American film.

A director named Raoul Walsh agreed. He and others believed the name was too feminine. Walsh would suggest that he take on that of a Revolutionary War general, Anthony Wayne. Ultimately "Anthony" was dropped in favor of "John."

The actor was not even present for the discussion.

Would he have enjoyed the same epic success as Marion Morrison? One will never know. It's reasonable to say, however, that even the most casual of movie lovers can't hear the name John Wayne without knowing who he was and have some sense of his impact on cinematic history.

Or, at least, they shouldn't. But this book is not about actors and movies. It's about patriotic leadership. The main word being the former.

One of the key lessons from Wayne's life is that it's ok to be a public figure and love your country. That's the visible and clear impact platform and patriotism can have. Too often, there is over celebration on the person, or what that individual portrays on stage or screen, not the ideals that are beneath the surface.

Wayne translated his exposure as an acclaimed actor into respect from the masses, not only for who and what he showed on the screen, but for his real-life actions as well.

Character Over Celebrity

A common myth about leadership, in any arena, is that a big, charismatic personality is required. With the current landscape of influencers aggressively attempting to gain followers, this idea may be even more prevalent, especially given the often-frantic gamesmanship of limitless posting in the pursuit of likes and comments.

History, at least here, tells a different story. John Wayne needed no internet to become an icon.

In an era predating the digital age's kaleidoscope of social media platforms, John Wayne carved out an authentic presence in American culture that transcended mere entertainment. Unlike today's carefully curated online personas, Wayne's patriotism emerged naturally through his work and public life, beginning with his breakthrough role in John Ford's "Stagecoach" (1939) and continuing through nearly 200 films over five decades.*

This began early as his fundamental beliefs were instilled at an early age. Raised Presbyterian, his first truths would be foundational and remain constant throughout his life as would his small-town values.

While he did not proselytize his faith, the associated convictions would quietly inform his ethics and choices. For Wayne, this was genuine, not for show or pretense. This does not mean, however, it was without blemish.

The authenticity of Wayne's patriotism resonated with audiences precisely because it wasn't performative—it was an extension of his genuine beliefs, even when those beliefs proved controversial. However, this observation comes with an important caveat: the man born Marion Morrison was neither purely the heroic figure of his Western films nor the flawless patriot some admirers imagined. His personal life included three marriages, and his political views, particularly regarding race relations and Indigenous peoples, reflect attitudes that many modern Americans find troubling.**

That is why there is an inherent danger in placing individuals, especially celebrities, on too high a pedestal. While

---

* Roberts, Randy, *John Wayne: American* (University of Nebraska Press, 1997).

** Bogdanovich, Peter. *John Wayne: The Last Interview* (Ballantine Books, 1999).

Wayne's love for America was genuine, and his characters strong, his private life was not spotless.

No reasonable person could make that claim.

There can be a sense that the veneer created either by virtue of their fame or in the mind of countless admirers is more than just that, appearance. John Wayne would have been the first to admit his flaws. Not just of himself, but the country he admired.

True patriotism is not ostentatious. It recognizes the faults and mistakes throughout our nation's history but can still be proud of who and what it stands for.

Is it also plausible that this can make for an even stronger and more authentic message for the general public? If there was one characteristic of Wayne's many portrayals, it was honesty. It was a trait that fans, friends, and family would grow to admire and remember about the actor and the man.

To say that fame can change a person is a given. Is it an absolute? Few things regarding this kind of work and life are. Again, this is why *character* matters over charisma. One can be faked and perceived as more real than is true. The other proves itself, at some point, for what it is, in the best and the worst of times.

*It's ok to be a public figure
and love your country.*

Rugged Individualism

The strength of any nation or community lies in its individualism and self-reliance. While that may, at face value, seem paradoxical, part of America's makeup is those who could stand on their own two feet (with God's help, of course).

Also, the idea of "pulling oneself up by their own bootstraps" may sound like a cliché, but the spirit behind it is real. Self-determination and grit are attributes found in many of the roles Wayne performed.

Undoubtably, he will likely always be associated with the American Cowboy and the pioneers who settled the Old West. Picture hopeful families and homesteaders traveling with a wagon train to start a new life thousands of miles from what they left behind.

Conditions could be brutal for those making the long and slow journey.

Weather was always a concern as sandstorms were common along the plains. Thunderstorms or even droughts could threaten as well. There was also the reality of disease, often fatal.

Many times, infected families were left behind to prevent spread.

And, of course, the presence of Native Americans, who believed these parties were crossing over sacred lands or cherished hunting ground, daily presented the very real potential for violent encounters.

Historian John D. Unruh Jr., in his definitive work on overland migration, documents that between 1840 and 1860, nearly 300,000 pioneers traversed the major trails westward.

His research reveals that the overlanders faced a complex array of natural and human challenges that transformed the journey into a severe test of physical endurance, psychological resilience, and communal cooperation.*

To say these families showed grit and determination would be an understatement. It is this kind of strength of character and perseverance Wayne portrayed on the screen.

Moviegoers were drawn to the toughness and gravel that resonated with every scene. It showed that it was reasonable to be both independent and interdependent at a time when both qualities were needed.

This is what remains so romantic and nostalgic about the Old West and why his characters connected in such a powerful way.

Code of the West

In Wayne's own words he said, *"A man's got to have a code, a creed to live by no matter his job."*

Everyone has that.

Behaving and relating from a set of guiding principles instead of trends, popular thought, feelings, or opinions is essential for leadership and for life. Because of his time on the movie screen, Wayne is often associated with what's commonly referred to as the *Code of the West*.

---

* Unruh Jr., John D. *The Plains Across: The Overland Emigrants and the Trans-Mississippi West, 1840-60* (University of Illinois Press, 1979), 408.

Because there was little, if any, actual law out on the range, an unwritten way of behavior was developed and observed as a means of maintaining survival and mutual respect. This was akin to a gentlemen's agreement, and, while not enforceable by law, this code was widely practiced by those wanting to avoid becoming a social outcast or pariah.

Historian Ramon Adams explains that the Code of the West emerged as an unwritten social contract among frontier inhabitants. As Adams notes, 'The Code was never written into the statutes, but it was respected with a quasi-religious dedication. It was a form of natural law that evolved from the requirements of range life and the character of the people who lived by it.*

Why the Cowboy Code Matters

Codes represent doctrines and values, not simply notions or ideas. While that may sound like splitting hairs, opinions can change and often do. Beliefs tend to be more entrenched and solid as roots are to a tree.

An apple tree is not going to grow pears. Whatever the root, it shows up in the fruit.

For the cowboy, as John Wayne would likely agree, this organic rule of law was grounded in an authentic truth for which people in the American West were willing to lay down their lives.

Film historian Paul O'Neil argues that Wayne's portrayal of Western characters wasn't just about entertainment, he was actively interpreting and transmitting these cultural codes to modern audiences. His films helped translate frontier ethics into contemporary leadership principles.**

---

* Adams, Ramon F, *The Old-Time Cowboy* (University of Oklahoma Press, 1961), 17.

** O'Neil, Paul, "The Western Code in Film: From Silver Screen to American Values." Film History Quarterly, Vol. 24, No. 2, 1978, 45-67.

This helped to create a distinctive culture that would speak to not only moviegoers but historians and succeeding generations.

Essentials from the Code of the West

What are the truisms and principles that can be applied from this "code"? After all, no set of guidelines or lessons has much value apart from impacting belief and behavior.

As mentioned, these were laws and ways to live that were more understood than legislated.

Author Zane Grey played a crucial role in codifying these principles in his 1934 novel *Code of the West*, giving formal structure to what had been unwritten rules. As Western historian Richard White explains, "The actual practices of frontier inhabitants became romanticized and structured into a formal 'code' through early twentieth-century literature and film, though the underlying values were rooted in authentic frontier experiences."***

Here are those "actual practices" that can still be lived today.

1) Live each day with courage.

Consider, for a moment, what life was like on the range and in untamed territory. Aside from the fact that there were no modern conveniences to ease their travel, as mentioned, dangers were clear and evident.

Historian Richard White also notes that courage on the frontier wasn't about bravado—it was about facing daily uncertainties with resolve. From weather to wildlife, every day required decisions that could mean life or death.****

*** White, Richard, *It's Your Misfortune and None of My Own: A New History of the American West* (University of Oklahoma Press, 1991), 315.

**** White, Richard, *It's Your Misfortune and None of My Own: A History of the American West* (Norman: University of Oklahoma Press, 1991), 45-46.

There is healthy fear, and then there can be a point in the mind where fear crosses over into something irrational and paralyzing.

Courage is not the absence of fear but taking reasonable action to overcome it, or, in John Wayne's own words, *"Courage is being scared to death but saddling up anyway."*

Every leader, if not every individual, faces a kind of fear and need for this kind of spirit. The chronicles of America are solidly marked with those who rose above their own personal terror to do the brave thing.

Every day calls for courage, and every day it can be found.

> *Courage is being scared to death*
> *and saddling up anyway.*
> —John Wayne

2) Take pride in your work.

According to Maslow, the highest motivating factor that anyone can attain in the work is self-actualization. As he articulated in his seminal work, self-actualization represents the full realization of one's potential, where work becomes an integral part of one's identity and purpose rather than merely a means to an end.*

That means what someone does, vocationally, correspondences with why they believe they are here on planet earth and part of their ultimate contribution. When that's the case, you can't help but take pride in your work and leadership.

That's not ego; that's nobility.

Those that understand what they do and how they contribute will long outlast themselves, will complete their

---

* Maslow, Abraham H, "A Theory of Human Motivation." *Psychological Review*, Vol. 50, No. 4, 1943, 370-396.

work from start to finish with a greater sense of excellence and devotion.

This is how great brands are built and sustained, including personal ones. Beyond logos, slogans, and flashy commercials, businesses and their leaders should be known for quality and a superior product.

American companies have been, and continue to be, successful not just because they know how to turn a profit, but because they grew customer loyalty by delivering a high value that represented often painstaking attention to detail.

Every organization and every worker, from the CEO to the junior accountant, should hold themselves responsible for that kind of standard.

Dr. Martin Luther King Jr. said, *"Whatever your life's work is, do it well. A man should do his job so well that the living, the dead, and the unborn could do it no better."*

Every day, one should operate and perform with a steadfast commitment to produce the best products and service he or she is able.

No one wants a soggy burger.

3) Always finish what you start.

History remembers those who finished, especially those who did so honorably and well. It also is checkered by those who imagined a great idea, wrote it down (maybe on a napkin) and never brought it to fruition.

The world is full of great starters. Not as many finishers.

Consider the Wright Brothers. Two bicycle repairmen who had an idea for a controlled flight and fought through what most would call failures, as well as freezing temperatures, to successfully fly an airplane on December 17th, 1903.

It's easy to look back at such dates, snapshots, even images, and either discount or neglect the very real trials and testing that went into what may seem, now, like an overnight success.

How many of these notable achievements would be lost to the ether of time had more chosen to not cross the finish line with their vision?

4) Do what has to be done.

There seems to be a simplicity and common-sense approach to this code. Again, this kind of thinking and doing was reflected in many of Wayne's roles. In fact, one of his wise quotes includes a title of one of the more notable films he made: *"True grit is making a decision and standing by it, doing what must be done."*

One of the definitions for *grit* includes *resolve*. Not only knowing what to do, but the actual execution. Resolutions are great but shouldn't be reserved only for the first of every year. Doing what has to be done is not optional depending on the day; at least, it shouldn't be. Resolve and sense of responsibility can speak every day and squelch feelings of apathy and complacency.

Those who settled the Old West couldn't afford the lure of laziness. The exceptional leader will not settle for it.

Know what you have to do. Do it. It's as simple as that.

5) Be tough but fair.

Leadership is not only just about influence. It also includes the caring commitment to empower and grow people.

As leadership scholars James M. Kouzes and Barry Z. Posner emphasize, the most effective leaders understand that leadership is a relationship, characterized by mutual respect and confidence. Leadership is not about imposing the leader's will but about engaging the hearts and minds of others.*

Truth and love must be given in equal measures.

---

* Kouzes, James M., and Barry Z. Posner. *The Leadership Challenge: How to Make Extraordinary Things Happen in Organizations*, 6th ed. (John Wiley & Sons, 2017), 30.

There are those in leadership positions who lean more to penalizing than caring equally about the person who made the mistake.

It is possible to be tough and tender. Many of Wayne's roles portrayed this balance as a celebrated and kind virtue.

Truth and love must be
given in equal measures.

6) When you make a promise, keep it.

Nothing destroys trust faster than broken promises.

Enough said.

7) Ride for the brand.

Icon is a word used for an individual who excels in a particular arena to the degree that they basically become the brand. John Wayne fits that category for the American Cowboy on screen. Tom Brady, with football, Babe Ruth, baseball, Hemingway as an author.

For the cowboy, the brand, burned into the hide of the skin of the animal, was everything. And because it identified to whom the cattle belonged, it also provided a way to protect the livestock and promote brand loyalty.

Cowboys would be willing to give their lives to protect their cattle and were proud of the outfit for which they rode.

8) Talk less and say more.

Many of John Wayne's characters were short on verbiage, long on action. It's an established truism that one speaks louder than the other.

Words absolutely matter, but increasing the number used does not guarantee the message will be any more effective. Would anyone really remember the Gettysburg Adress, or at least the first few lines, had it not been as concise as it was?

It's easy to picture these cowboys, and Wayne, as those who didn't talk a lot but said much when they did, then validated their words by their deeds.

9) Remember that some things aren't for sale.

People often lack a clear understanding of the definition or idea of *conviction*. Much of what is embraced or espoused, even to the point of driving one's life, can be narrowed to more of a belief, at most, or, at the least, simply opinion.

The latter can change. It often does.

Convictions are more life and death. Some people can't be bought, nor can their ideals. Consider the implications of this truism. Great lives and even greater causes are built on deep convictions and strong character.

One can give and compromise on anything other than principle.

That should never be up for sale.

10) Know where to draw the line.

Similar to #9, everyone experiences "line in the sand" moments that force a decision or particular response.

When seen on screen or read in a late chapter of a favorite book, one can almost hear the music in the background as these instances can be quite intense. In fact, legend has it that this phrase, "draw the line," comes from the fatal battle at the Alamo when Colonel William Travis drew a line in the sand upon being told to surrender by the Mexican troops.

He was warned that if he failed to do so, his entire regiment would be killed.

Travis asked his men to make a decision and take a stand: to choose their fate by which side of the line they would take.

All those who fought defending the Alamo died.

That part of the story is absolutely true. Whether or not Travis drew an actual line in the sand, his men certainly did with their lives.

These stories, and more, are emblematic of the characters John Wayne famously portrayed.

It is why he is remembered in the way he is, a legend of the American West, resolute, gritty, and honest, representing the best parts of what made that rugged age important to the history of a young nation.

On screen, John Wayne was larger than life. His characters were strong and rooted in strong character. While his life away from his acting may have been dotted with imperfections, his portrayal of authentic patriotism still represented the value of character over charisma.

Wayne's internal pledge to live by a personal code, showing pride in his work, balancing a tough aura with tenderness and fairness, exemplifies a leadership grounded in values and steady actions. No leader is perfect, nor was Wayne. Embracing that truth helps one live and lead with authenticity, resiliency, and grace.

That's better than any movie script or Hollywood ending.

Wayne's Leadership Principles

★ **Portray Authentic Patriotism:** Wayne demonstrated you can love your country while acknowledging its flaws. True leaders balance pride with honest recognition of what needs improvement.

★ **Transcend Celebrity for Substance:** Wayne's influence came from his values, not his fame. Real leadership flows from character rather than superficial popularity or charm.

★ **Live Your Personal Code:** Wayne didn't just play heroes—he embodied core principles on and off screen. Leaders must stand for something beyond situational convenience.

★ **Elevate Production Values:** Whether in films or business ventures, Wayne demanded excellence in execution. Leaders raise standards in everything they touch.

★ **Be Tough but Fair:** Wayne's screen persona combined toughness with compassion, showing that true authority doesn't sacrifice humanity.

★ **Honor Simple Truths:** Despite his sophistication, Wayne championed basic virtues—courage, honesty, loyalty. Leaders shouldn't overcomplicate timeless principles.

★ **Embrace Your Imperfections:** Wayne understood his life wasn't flawless, making his example more authentic. Real leaders acknowledge their humanity while striving for better.

Chapter Six

Michael Jordan – American Athlete

"I've never lost a game. I just ran out of time."

—Michael Jordan

GOAT. No, not the animal, of course.

This is the acronym used to designate the greatest of all time, primarily in a given sport.

While that designation, at first glance, may seem subjective, it is widely accepted and can be supported with certain facts and statistics.

Few, in all the pantheon of not only NBA history, but sports itself, match this description as much as Michael Jeffrey Jordan.

His name is synonymous with not only basketball glory, but the drive, determination, and spirit of excellence needed to achieve the kind of success only a few players would ever see.

While talent and ability are clearly essential ingredients in the realization of such a pinnacle, true winners know that's not nearly enough. Further, while his accomplishments speak for themselves, what may do so more quietly is the kind of fortitude and resilience demonstrated by an aspiring young player who was cut from his varsity team in high school.

It was the same kind of grit and determination that not only led to Jordan's many sports victories and championships but also helped him continue to step into a batter's box, struggling to get hits, while playing in the minor leagues of baseball with a hitting average of around .200.

That kind of will shows up not just in the wins, but in how an athlete deals with the non-victorious seasons that are a part of *every* journey.

Regardless, statistics help to tell a story and, again, validate the high esteem placed on one who would be remembered as the greatest individual of note in any sport.

According to Roland Lazenby's definitive biography, Jordan's career achievements are unparalleled in basketball history.*

★ Jordan led the Chicago Bulls to six NBA championships (1991–1993 and 1996–1998), including two "three-peats," winning every NBA Finals series he entered.

★ He earned five NBA Most Valuable Player awards (1988, 1991, 1992, 1996, and 1998), demonstrating his sustained excellence over a decade.

★ His fourteen NBA All-Star selections reflected his consistent dominance in the league, representing the best of the Eastern Conference.

★ Jordan claimed ten scoring titles and was named NBA Defensive Player of the Year in 1988, notably

---

* Lazenby, Roland. *Michael Jordan: The Life* (Little, Brown and Company, 2014), 201-205.

achieving the rare triple crown of MVP, Scoring Champion, and Defensive Player of the Year in that same season.

★ Before his professional career, he played three seasons with the North Carolina Tar Heels, securing an NCAA championship in 1982.

★ He won two Olympic Gold Medals (1984 and 1992), with the latter coming as part of the legendary "Dream Team" in Barcelona.

Perspectives may vary when examining this kind of data, as it relates to a career in sports, but even the casual observer should recognize the extreme dedication required and demanded to reach this level of legendary status.

An American Sportsman for an American Sport

Basketball is an American game, though it was created by a Canadian, James Naismith, a physical education instructor. It was designed to be less impactful on the body than football.

Professional basketball can trace its roots back to 1898 with the formation of the National Basketball League. While it was crude, and much different than what would follow with the American League and the NBA, it set a solid stage for an elite plane of competition for decades.

Though it could be argued that, as a sport, basketball may not capture national attention to the extent of baseball or even football, it remains a unique and beloved part of American athletic history with a dedicated fan base.

No doubt Naismith could hardly imagine a rudimentary game that included a *literal basket* would spawn a sport not limited to the professional arena, or even the country of origin.

Basketball is an international phenomenon as much as it is the friendly pickup game in any backyard of Maintown, USA or anywhere in the world.

Not Making the Cut

While it can be hard to imagine that the person most would consider the greatest basketball player to have ever graced the court could be cut from any team, as has already been mentioned, that's exactly what happened to the one many refer to as MJ.

In 1978, long before he was a household name, Michael Jordan was a sophomore at Emsley A. Laney High School, trying desperately to make the varsity team.

With only fifteen spots available, Jordan's chances were not helped by the fact that he could not yet make a dunk, partially due to his small stature of only 5'10".

His friend, and fellow sophomore, Leroy Smith *did* make it, ironically for the same reason Jordan did not, *height*. Jordan would find himself later that day locked in his room, crying.

This would be a natural reaction of any youth disappointed by not making the cut, but perhaps this is where the seeds of greatness began to germinate for Michael Jordan, as defeat would fuel desire.

Letdown would spur motivation, not misery.

Blooming Where Planted

Jordan would go on to be a star on the Junior Varsity Team, regularly scoring forty points a night. If there was a chip on his shoulder, it seems to have helped him in all things basketball. Crowds were amazed at this display of talent and scoring ability from a member of the JV squad.

Could the varsity coach have gotten it wrong? Either way, Michael Jordan discovered, early, the drive to succeed and work to exceed expectations on the basketball court.

Speaking of growth, over the summer Jordan would begin to morph, and in 1979, he grew four inches, helping him to finally make the varsity team in his junior year. Securing the spot might cause the average player to relax. But Michael

Jordan was never that type of individual. In fact, he worked just as hard, if not harder, and would average more than twenty points a game.

In his senior year, he would lead his team to a 19-4 record, averaging a triple-double and being named a McDonald's All-American.

"His greatness" was blooming.

Coaching All-Star Potential

Traditionally, Dean Smith, the late coach of the University of North Carolina Tarheels, had a rule or standing policy that he did not play freshmen.

This was mentioned during recruiting visits so as to not unduly get players' hopes up.

Dean Smith's system was not designed for freshmen to star. In fact, Smith was known for bringing his first-year players along slowly, making sure they understood the fundamentals before giving them significant playing time.*

Michael Jordan started on his *very first game*.

Could this have been a glimpse of things to come? Given the fact that he would average 13.5 points per game, it would be hard to argue otherwise. The North Carolina Tarheels were perennial championship contenders for years under Smith, and shining bright along elite players like James Worthy and Sam Perkins was no small feat.

But that's exactly what Jordan was able to do.

---

* Smith, Dean. *A Coach's Life: My Forty Years in College Basketball* (Random House, 2002).

But would that have happened to the degree it did without the mentorship and leadership of Coach Smith? Jordan didn't seem to think so. What would lead to one of the most indelible moments in Tarheel Basketball history, as well as in all college sports, were a lot of other moments that were not so grand but were necessary to build success.

Coaching is a vital role for every leader. This was no exception. Talent doesn't rule over good coaching; it *benefits* from it.

Did Dean Smith see all the growing potential that was inside this rising star who wore number 23? Maybe it didn't matter. Good coaches bring out the best in players, regardless of what that best may be.

Talent doesn't rule over good coaching;
it benefits from it.

The respect and admiration that was offered to one by the other was mutual. Smith admired Jordan's work ethic and pursuit of excellence, and the latter would go on to see his coach as a second father, alluding that he taught him about more than just basketball.

It could be roundly considered that the two are intertwined. The college experience for any athlete can be one that includes pseudo-parenting as students are often far from home.

Regardless, Jordan certainly benefited from Smith's guidance, as did his team.

Fifteen Seconds

Every sport has its championships, and college is certainly no exception. While some seem more popular than others, perhaps due to the type of game played, all have their own brand of excitement and ultimate glory.

The NCAA Tournament can trace its beginnings all the way back to 1939 and has grown to be one of the biggest sporting events in America, if not across the world. Known as "March Madness" for the time of year in which it takes place, it has grown in lore due to its upsets and the overall legacy created by many notable teams throughout the years and decades.

Teams like Kentucky, UCLA, Indiana, Duke, and, yes, North Carolina are among those that have cemented their place in the history of this event.

In the 1981 season, the UNC Tarheels were pursuing their second of what would eventually become six national championships to date. As a side note, this was significant to Dean Smith's reputation, as it was said by many that he was not able to win "the big one," despite other examples of success during this time at North Carolina.

Flash forward to March 29th, 1982, and the title game of the NCAA Men's Basketball Tournament. With any such final matchup, the records don't really matter.

Nor does the half-time score.

In fact, as was proven on this night, a lead can at least be somewhat dubious until the game clock reaches the final second of the second half.

The Tarheels' opposing team, Georgetown, only needed to outlast their opponents fifteen more of those precious ticks to win. But the player who once couldn't even make the Varsity team at his high school took the shot that would prove that as long as there was time, there was a chance to win.

Basketball geeks and historians of the game would analyze and dissect the play that was designed and mention the fact that James Worthy actually had a better game statistically and was the one of the more likely choices to make the play.

Seth Davis gives the nod to another player. The primary option was actually Sam Perkins on the wing, but Georgetown overplayed it, leaving Michael open. That moment would become one of the most significant in NCAA championship history.*

The pass, and the chance to win the game, went to number 23, who before that shot was known as Mike Jordan. Afterward he would forever be referred to as Michael.

Changing the NBA

Upon being selected third by the Chicago Bulls in the 1984 NBA Draft, expectations were high but not unreasonable. There is always a tension and some level of stress in the uncertainty that exists between the anticipation, and eventual reality, of drafting rookie players to any team.

---

* Davis, Seth, *When March Went Mad: The Game That Transformed Basketball* (Times Books, 2009).

Draft busts do occasionally happen.

Not the case with number 23. His playing style and likeability would bring not only wins, but more fans into the stadium. Nike signed him to a shoe deal for "Air Jordans," a branded sneaker that technically he was not allowed to wear, subject to fines.

He would often stick out his tongue, which became a part of his personal style, as he would dazzle on and off the court. Any doubts that Jordan would be the elite player that was anticipated were silenced with a stellar rookie season that led to his first All-Star appearance in 1985.

In the fifteen years of his NBA career, Michael Jordan not only dominated the game of basketball, he transformed it.

Jordan's impact transcended basketball. By the mid-1990s, he had become the most recognized athlete in the world, with a global marketing presence that redefined athlete endorsements.*

---

* Andrews, David L, *Michael Jordan, Inc.: Corporate Sport, Media Culture, and Late Modern America* (SUNY Press, 2001).

But more than money, his influence reverberates and continues to inspire future, and hopeful, professional basketball players.

That's legacy at its best.

Playing Sick

Every leader, manager, or supervisor understands the reality of needing to provide cover or a substitute when someone calls in sick. What one hopes is that the team member is truthful and not suffering from the Monday blues or, perhaps, a morning hangover.

Playing sick or hurt is not an unfamiliar circumstance for athletes, especially given the situation or stakes that may be involved. For preseason games, or if there is a twenty-point lead, many coaches would sit their best players in order to protect them from further injury or simply let them rest.

June 11th, 1997, game five of the NBA Finals, forever known as "The Flu Game," offered neither of those two scenarios. Michael Jordan's performance, under extreme duress, would become one of the most unforgettable moments in the league's history and further cement his elite status as the greatest to ever play the game of basketball.

While it was ultimately proven to not be the flu, but, interestingly enough, food poisoning from bad pizza, the reality is that he still played sick. It could be argued that it would, of course, make sense to do so given that his team was pursuing an NBA title.

Perhaps.

Or maybe that's just the kind of competitor Michael Jordan was.

Statistics support both theories. Scoring thirty-eight points (including the tie breaker at the end of the game) and playing for forty-four minutes is reflective of someone who is either physically fine or valiantly playing through an ailment.

History supports the latter. In fact, according to team physician Dr. John Hefferon, Jordan's temperature had reached 103 degrees during the game.* Jordan muscled his way through the game and on to help the Chicago Bulls' secure their fifth NBA Championship.

This transcends basketball. This was one man's steely resolve, refusing to bow to his body's limits.

And for all the world to see.

Leadership On and Off the Court

While there is simply too much history of this American athlete for just one chapter, there can be an equal number of lessons that one can use as inspiration to elevate his or her leadership game.

Michael Jordan was not only a star athlete, he was also a strong, if often aggressive, leader. While some on his team would bristle at his sharp communications and tactics that could be perceived as intense and intimidating, it was all about winning and competing at your highest level, given your particular skill set and abilities.

Individual greatness is amplified when it makes others successful. Michael Jordan put the fear in his opponents and brought out the best in his teammates.

That requires a leader, and Jordan proved that in many ways.

Hard Work

As mentioned, talent is not enough. History is full of talented people who were just plain lazy. Their names are obscure or

---

** Porter, David L, *Michael Jordan: A Biography* (Greenwood Press, 2007).

unknown because they failed to achieve as they refused to work hard enough or at all.

Ability does not afford entitlement. One has to put in time and effort to be successful and model that for others. Jordan would spend countless hours in the gym, often past the comfort and commitment level of his teammates. But that's the model of a leader who inspires. High-performance teams have high expectations.

Standards matter. Jordan's were kept high, and he expected everyone on the team to at least work as hard as he.

Not everyone did, but the example was clearly set.

The Value of Team

While Jordan was immensely talented and a once-in-a-lifetime athlete, he could not win basketball games single-handedly. John Wooden was known to say *it takes ten hands to win on the court*. As exceptional as he was, he was still only *one* member of the Chicago Bulls. There were fourteen other teammates who could have a hand in winning (or losing) on any given day.

Would there have been six NBA championships without Scottie Pippen? Or Steve Kerr, or even John Paxton? Teamwork can be such an overused term that it can feel almost meaningless. It can be as lifeless as the quote on a motivation poster seen in almost any corporate office complex.

Consider the power, though, of the greatest athlete of all time not only recognizing, but employing, the reality of leveraging the skills and acumen of his fellow players to reach the kind of heights he could never reach alone.

That kind of spirit must be fostered. For leaders, that requires humility and a shrunken ego. As mentioned, Michael Jordan will be remembered as the greatest of all time until someone else wrests that mantel away.

But it was the Chicago Bulls who earned those six titles. Jordan's greatness did not exist without his teammates. It complemented, and was complemented by, those who contributed on the floor.

Individual greatness is amplified
when it makes others successful.

A Now Focus

All athletes need a short memory. A dropped pass, interception, missed field goal, unforced error, strikeout, these are all letdowns in player's experience that can morph into a slump, physical, psychological, and emotional. While Jordan was a champion, many times over, clearly not every game resulted in victory. Not every shot went through the basket.

Here is how Jordan described it: *"I've missed more than 9000 shots in my career. I've lost almost 300 games. 26 times, I've been trusted to take the game winning shot and missed. I've failed over and over and over again in my life. And that is why I succeeded."*

80% of that quote is about missing and losing. How can it then be said that it is what leads to success? Jordan understood, as many do, losing can only be permanent if it robs one of present focus. No one would easily mark Micheal Jordan as a loser. It's a label too many wear, fatal for the leader.

Every individual, team, organization, and community has failed or missed the mark.

But what of the present focus? Is the failure a blip? Something to use as a lesson? Or does it become a sentence that has no ending? True champions choose the former.

Michael Jordan was that kind of competitor and champion. His work ethic and ideals match the same kind of hard work and tenacity that other athletes share in the world of sports entertainment.

Even for the casual observer or those who don't follow basketball, Michael Jordan is an individual worth following. He overcame early and repeated failures in a constant pursuit of excellence. His work ethic was unquestionable and a clear example for others to follow.

It only solidified and bolstered the argument that he was, and is, the greatest of all time and a model for pursuing the best in self and team.

Whether it was leading the Chicago Bulls to championship after championship or proudly playing for his country in the Olympics, Jordan proved that single accomplishments and team success are not mutually exclusive.

His competitiveness may have ruffled a few feathers, but also motivated everyone around him to work harder, aim higher, and demand more from themselves than they might not have otherwise. In this way, he demonstrated a tremendous leadership lesson: Real champions do not just elevate self, but everyone around them.

Michael Jordan truly was, and is, the greatest in every sense of the word, both on and off the court.

Jordan's Leadership Principles

★ **Rise Above Rejection:** Jordan transformed being cut from his high school team into unstoppable motivation. True leaders use setbacks as springboards to greatness.

★ **Perfect Through Relentless Practice:** Jordan's legendary work ethic in the gym reshaped what was possible in basketball. Leaders must outwork everyone, even when they're already the best.

★ **Elevate Your Entire Team:** Despite his individual brilliance, Jordan learned to make everyone around him better. Real leaders multiply their impact through others.

★ **Focus on the Present:** Jordan never let past failures or successes affect his current performance. Leaders stay locked in on the immediate challenge.

★ **Set and Model Standards:** Jordan didn't just demand excellence—he demonstrated it daily. Leaders establish expectations through personal example.

★ **Remain Coachable Always:** Even as the greatest player, Jordan continued learning from coaches like Dean Smith. True leaders never stop growing.

★ **Play Through Pain:** The "Flu Game" showed Jordan's ability to transcend physical limits. Leaders find ways to deliver when circumstances are harshest.

Chapter Seven

Amelia Earhart – American Aviator

"Don't wait. The time will never be just right."

—Amelia Earhart

Aviation is a man's world.

At least, that was the predominant school of thought when Amelia Earhart decided she would aim to fly. While her interest began sometime in the late 1910s, her first lesson was in 1921.

This was a time following the first World War, the beginning of the Roaring Twenties. And while aviation was still relatively young, it had accelerated quite dramatically during the war.

Commercial flights began in the U.S. in 1914. Postal airmail was established in the late 1910s and early 1920s. There were also the "barnstorming" events at which pilots would perform stunts, even giving rides at fairs and other similar outdoor events.

According to Dorothy Cochrane, curator at the National Air and Space Museum, in the 1920s, aviation was transforming from a dangerous sport to a more reliable form of transportation, though it remained a male-dominated field.*

As far as the overall technology of aircrafts, most were biplanes with open cockpits. And while the engines and the structures themselves were becoming surer and more stable, navigation was still quite rudimentary.

Regardless, even in this early era of flying, records were being set for distances, speed, and even altitude. Charles Lindbergh would make his historic transatlantic flight in 1927.

Clearly, there was great curiosity and enthusiasm in the world of man-made flight that first burst on the scene in Kitty Hawk, North Carolina, that fateful 17th day in December 1903.

Flying was new, exciting, and here to stay.

Imagine how the reality of what was possible was already being tested and expanded. Many were doing just that. While the novelty of it all was still present, the focus would begin to transition in very real and practical ways and continuous, rapid development.

This would be the world Amelia Earhart would choose to enter, but not without significant setbacks and a lot of pluck. It would require all of her love for flying and desire to make her mark as a true American aviator to see her through to all that she wanted to achieve, one of the biggest challenges being her gender.

---

* Cochrane, Dorothy, *Pioneers of Flight: Women in Early Aviation* (Smithsonian Press, 2018), 127.

That's not to say that because she was female she couldn't fly. History already says otherwise. However, in this particular era, it is estimated that there were only about 200 female licensed pilots in the U.S. and perhaps only a few dozen internationally.

Again, this was not a reflection of ability, only the societal norm at the time. Stereotypes are always lazy, in any generation or era.

But it *was* the cultural environment in which Amelia Earhart lived. The "man's world" acceptance was not limited to the profession of flying. Women faced barriers far and wide as their value was often tied to appearance and delicacy, not physical strength, emotional intelligence, or mental acuity.

This makes what Earhart was able to accomplish all the more exceptional.

Climbing Trees—Made for Adventure

In the wide-open spaces of Atchison, Kansas, a young Amelia Earhart could be found hunting, collecting insects, and climbing trees. There was a day this behavior would be deemed as tomboyish, another bygone term, but one useful for those who understood the reference at the time.

Her mother would even dress her and her sister in bloomers rather than dresses to allow them more freedom to play as they wanted.

Earhart would learn how to have an independent and determined streak as her family moved constantly due to her father's battle with alcohol, which would subsequently result in loss of steady employment.

She would need to constantly adapt. This trait, as well as a dogged determination, would serve her well in her pursuits.

"Flying" Down a Ramp

When she was approximately seven years old, she and her sister constructed a ramp that would extend beyond the roof of her grandparents' shed.

One can guess who would be the first to test it.

A brave Amelia would climb up and onto the roof with a wooden box in her hand that would serve as a sort of cart. After getting inside, she would thrillingly push herself down the ramp, fully expecting the makeshift rollercoaster to function, at least adequately.

It did not.

Flying off the ramp, the cart, or box, would eventually tumble onto the ground, with Amelia still inside. Instead of tears and terror, the reaction, even with bruises and scrapes, was exhilaration.

History does not record if there was a second attempt. One can only surmise.

The First Encounter and Beyond

Who knows what will spark a love or passion for a thing? For each person, the impetus or incitement can be as varied as the person or their fascinations.

But something clicked when, while living in Toronto, Canada, during WWI, Amelia Earhart would spend time watching the pilots of the Royal Flying Corps at a nearby training facility. Captivated, perhaps she was already envisioning herself in a cockpit enjoying the same open-air exhilaration.

She was twenty years old at the time.

Though she didn't immediately pursue flying, the flickering flame would continue to kindle when she was able to receive her first plane ride, years later. Pilot Frank Hawks would provide the experience in Long Beach, California in 1920.

Upon remembering the event, Earhart would say that the experience of that first flight changed her life forever. As Earhart later wrote in her journal, *"After that flight, I knew I myself had to fly."**

Passion locks one in and seldom lets go.

It should come as no surprise that her excitement grew and grew quickly. Earhart would begin working odd jobs to raise enough money for flying lessons, which would begin early January 1921 with a female aviator, Anita "Neta" Snook.

Earhart would prove to be quite the quick learner and apt student.

According to aviation historian Doris L. Rich, under Snook's tutelage, Earhart demonstrated remarkable aptitude for flying. She absorbed technical information quickly and showed unusual steadiness in handling the aircraft. Within just a few months, she was already performing advanced maneuvers that typically challenged more experienced pilots.**

Consider the wonderment of someone who has been awestruck by the idea of piloting a plane to be sitting in the cockpit, edging ever closer to her dream.

Another tangible step towards that aim, and to further immersing herself in the world of aviation, Earhart purchased her first plane in 1921. It was second hand, a Kinner Airstair biplane, and she lovingly nicknamed it "The Canary" because of the bright yellow color with which it was adorned.

It was this aircraft that Earhart would use to set her first women's record by rising to an altitude of 14,000 feet, a foretaste of more exploits to come.***

---

* Butler, Susan, *East to the Dawn: The Life of Amelia Earhart* (Da Capo Press, 2009), 89.

** Rich, Doris L., *Amelia Earhart: A Biography* (Smithsonian Institution Press, 1989), 42.

*** Lovell, Mary S., *The Sound of Wings: The Life of Amelia Earhart* (St. Martin's Press, 1989), 104.

Passion locks one in and seldom lets go.

Pushing Boundaries

To break any record requires a fight with gravity, much like flying itself.

As Henry Ford stated, *"Remember that the airplane takes off against the wind, not with it."*

While that may sound cliché, it's certainly apropos for Amelia Earhart.

Of course, she was aware of the inherent limits any would-be female pilot would face, in addition to the learning curve presented to all aviators.

Perhaps it was because she was aware and balanced that knowledge against her dream of adding yet another name to the small list of female pilots that she found the grit necessary to not only push those boundaries, but smash through.

This would become formalized as she received her official pilot's license in May of 1923 from the Fédération Aéronautique Internationale (FAI), only the sixteenth woman to do so from this body.

This had to be a thrill and a sense of exhilarated achievement. It can almost be certain that Earhart believed this was an opportunity she valiantly climbed just as she did those trees as a child, or the open sky as she would gain altitude to greater and greater heights.

As mentioned, it was expected that women would not pursue these kinds of dreams. Leaders, however, don't bend to societal norms; they break them or start new ones.

For Amelia was now a licensed pilot, and the sky was the limit.

More Records and Transatlantic Flights

While flying across oceans and from one country to another is common to the modern traveler, remember the context of the 1920s era.

Advances *did* continue to be made, but the limit of aviation was still bound by the times. However, it was due to, or in spite of, these limitations that many pilots, including Earhart, would continue to seek to go beyond the edge and break new ground.

And records.

These would be many and varied, all demonstrating Earheart's love for flying as well as the same daring that prompted her to get in a box and slide down a homemade ramp on her grandparents' tool shed.

According to Butler's definitive biography of Earhart, her remarkable achievements transformed aviation history in rapid succession.*

In 1928, she became the first woman to cross the Atlantic by air as a passenger aboard the "Friendship," completing the journey in 20 hours and 40 minutes. The following year, she placed third in the inaugural Women's Air Derby, popularly known as the "Powder Puff Derby." By 1930, she had set a new women's speed record of 181 mph.

Her most celebrated achievement came in 1932 when she became the first woman to fly solo across the Atlantic, completing the journey in 14 hours and 56 minutes. That same year, she accomplished two more firsts: completing the first solo non-stop transcontinental flight by a woman from Los Angeles to Newark in approximately 19 hours and becoming the first woman to fly solo in an autogiro.

---

* Butler, Susan, *East to the Dawn: The Life of Amelia Earhart* (Da Capo Press, 2009), 281-289.

In 1935, Earhart continued to break records, becoming the first person to fly solo from Hawaii to California, covering 2,408 miles in 18 hours and 16 minutes. She followed this with two more pioneering solo flights: from Los Angeles to Mexico City, and a non-stop journey from Mexico City to Newark.

Many, many *firsts*.

It probably shouldn't be underestimated or understated how significant it is to be the first in something worth celebrating. Those who set precedents can be a model for those who would follow. George Washington is remembered as the nation's patriarch, not only because he was the first president, but also how he modeled how an individual in that office should lead and behave.

The breaking of the sound barrier was celebrated as well as the first to man to the moon.

The world of sports is a plethora of firsts that propel star athletes to halls of fame. The cynic might try to argue that Amelia Earhart had fame in mind, but the sense of history seems to offer a different story and perspective.

Leaders…don't bend to societal norms,
they break them or start new ones.

Amelia Earhart simply wanted to fly and do so above and beyond any man-made or internal barriers.

Hers was a story of courageously taking to the skies.

That Courage Tested

Every solo flight that Amelia Earhart undertook could be considered historic in some way due to the fact that there were so few women making them. More than one such flight was noteworthy, and not necessarily because of its success, but more the near miss and peril.

On May 29th, 1932, Amelia would set out to become the first woman to fly solo nonstop across the Atlantic Ocean.

Nestled securely in her single-engine Lockheed Vega 5B, Earhart would take off with favorable conditions to traverse the expected 2,000 miles from Harbor Grace, Newfoundland, Canada, to Paris France.

As clear as the sky was at the time, so was the vision and anticipation of the successful completion of what was still considered a tremendous feat for any pilot.

At some point, about twelve hours in, the weather would take a turn and begin to deteriorate. Storms are no stranger to any seasoned aviator. However, heavy winds and rain were a different adversary for the pilots of the 1920s and 1930s than today.

Due to a plane's structure, instrumentation, and mechanical makeup at the time, a storm created much more alarm than what is common today. Earhart's altimeter had stopped working, making it difficult to gauge her altitude. She also noticed her plane was leaking fuel.

Storms can come in many shapes and sizes, which determine the steps a pilot will take to navigate and survive. Earhart herself would say, *"The most difficult thing is the decision to act. The rest is merely tenacity. The fears are paper tigers. You can do anything."*

This can serve as a powerful metaphor for life, work, and leadership.

But what about *during* the storm? Decisive action is needed then. To be caught in a storm with yet thousands of miles yet to go must have been harrowing.

As the storm worsened, the plane was easily tossed by turbulence. As she would later describe the experience, *"I did not know how long I could keep up this terrific struggle with the elements."*

Despite the challenges, she maintained her composure and kept flying.

What other choice is there? No pilot can control the weather. No individual can control circumstance, only how much calm he or she can find in the midst of it and how to best come out on the other side.

This is all the more incredible as Earhart also described part of the experience this way:

"The plane was almost on its back. Once I felt it rise, I had the breath-taking impression that it was looping."

While the original destination was Paris, France, the storm simply would not allow that.

Realizing this, Earhart decided to land at the first viable place. This turned out to be near Londonderry, Northern Ireland, to the surprise of several cows in the area. One can only imagine the balance of thought and perspective upon completion of a trip that became wrought with danger and did not reach its original goal.

History says that Earhart took it in stride and in a way that reflected her modesty, not to mention humor, as she *"pulled up in a farmer's back yard."*

Despite the setbacks, the feat was lauded worldwide as she did, indeed, become the first woman to fly solo across the Atlantic, and only the second person to do so, following

Charles Lindbergh. Earhart's solo transatlantic flight in 1932 wasn't just about breaking records—it demonstrated that women could handle the most challenging aspects of aviation just as capably as men.*

This is simply another example of a determined spirit going against the wind. It also helped set her apart and would elevate her status as one of the preeminent aviators of her time, if not in all of American lore.

Mastery and Mystery

While her 1932 transatlantic flight was mostly a success, a shroud of mystery remains enveloped around her last one.

This, in 1937, would be an attempt to circumnavigate the globe, a distance of approximately 29,000 miles, in a Lockheed Electra 10E, an aircraft specially modified for long-distance.

With her, to help plot the course, was Fred Noonan, an experienced sea captain and navigator.

After departing on June 1st, by the 29th of that same month they had completed approximately 22,000 miles, reaching Lae, New Guinea. The final leg of the trip would be the most challenging as it would seek to cross over 2,500 miles of open water.

---

* Corn, Joseph J., *The Winged Gospel: America's Romance with Aviation* (Johns Hopkins University Press, 2002), 173.

As with any elongated flight, especially one of this magnitude, communication with outside resources and assets was vitally important. Because of that, the U.S. Coast Guard had stationed the Itasca, a cutter, near Howland Island to assist through radio if needed.

Fate would have it, though, that there were issues with the on-air exchange between Earhart and the ship. She could hear the Itasca, but the Itasca could not hear her clearly. If ever there was a time in which that situation would have been needed in reverse, or not at all, it was this one.

At 7:42 a.m. (local time) Earhart transmitted, *"We must be on you but cannot see you—but gas is running low. Have been unable to reach you by radio. We are flying at 1,000 feet."*

Her last known communication, at 8:43, was, *"We are on the line 157 337. We will repeat this message. We will repeat this on 6,210 kilocycles."*

"Wait."

Much speculation has been offered for Earhart's use of the word "wait."

Perhaps she was preparing to transmit again and needed to switch frequencies. Maybe she was having to conserve battery power and decided to pause communications. She and Noonan may have been preparing for an emergency procedure.

This is just part of what would be the mysterious circumstances of Earhart's final flight. Whatever the prompting for this last word in her last radio transmission, history cryptically describes what happened next.

Amelia Earhart was never seen or heard from again.

A Vanished Legend

The disappearance of Amelia Earhart remains one of America's most enduring mysteries. According to Elgen and Marie Long's definitive research, it has generated more ongoing speculation and research than almost any other missing-person case in aviation history.*

Several theories abound as to exactly what happened to one of the world's most famous pilots:

- **She crashed**: The plane simply ran out of fuel and fell into the ocean.

- **Island Theory**: They were able to reach Gardner Island (now Nikumaroro) and died as castaways.

- **Captured**: The two were captured by the Japanese, this theory being one of the most discredited.

The U.S. Government did launch the largest and most expensive air and sea rescue in history to attempt to find Earhart and her navigator, to no avail.

No trace of the aircraft, or its crew, was ever found.

Does the tragic and inexplicable end of this attempted journey detract or amplify the life and exploits of Amelia Earhart?

Most would likely answer the latter.

The tale of her final flight has helped to keep her story alive and serves not only as a matter of great mystery, but further research and exploration.

Amelia Earhart continues to inspire beyond whatever grave in which she finally rested.

Much like the spirit of a nation, Amelia Earhart sought to soar with a freedom and determination to elevate and push boundaries.

While Earhart did not begin the trend of female pilots, through her achievements and adventures, she would advance it like few others. She would be a champion in advocating for women in aviation, including wartime.

---

* Long, Elgen M. and Marie K. Long, *Amelia Earhart: The Mystery Solved* (Simon & Schuster, 2000), 216-220.

Her courage in the face of adversity, both in the sky and on the ground, offers lessons in determination and grit any leader can follow.

Amelia Earhart was, above all, a pioneer.

In a world in which the norms for her desired vocation were essentially filled and preset, this brave pilot would ultimately leave her impression and thumbprint on America's identity as one who ventured to chart new territory and prove what's possible.

Her story is much more than her tragic disappearance. Her record of high achievement should not be overshadowed by her uncertain end. Amelia Earhart can be remembered as a fearless and undaunted spirit who broke barriers, not just for herself, but for every female aviator who would follow.

This pursuit of individuality and chasing new and epic horizons is a powerful reminder that leadership is not about quietly existing in confined spaces but breaking out and redefining what society considered normal and safe.

Amelia Earhart had more than enough talent and courage to soar with that idea.

Earhart's Leadership Principles

★ **Break Convention Boldly:** Earhart shattered gender barriers and societal limitations. Like Ford, true leaders don't accept artificial constraints—they transcend them.

★ **Channel Passion into Purpose:** Earhart's love of flying drove her to achievement. Authentic passion fuels the perseverance needed for breakthrough accomplishments.

★ **Weather Through Storms:** During her harrowing 1932 flight, Earhart maintained composure despite failing equipment and severe weather. Leaders stay steady when circumstances turn turbulent.

★ **Chart a Course for Others:** By succeeding in a male-dominated field, Earhart created opportunities for countless others. Real leaders don't just achieve—they open doors.

★ **Balance Risk with Preparation:** Every record Earhart broke was preceded by careful preparation. Bold action requires both daring and deliberate planning.

★ **Practice Grace Under Pressure:** When forced to land in Ireland instead of Paris, Earhart responded with humor. Leaders maintain perspective when plans go awry.

★ **Build a Lasting Legacy:** Earhart's advocacy for women's advancement influenced generations. True leadership impact echoes far beyond immediate achievements.

Chapter Eight

Mark Twain – American Author

"Loyalty to country ALWAYS.
Loyalty to government, when it deserves it."

—Mark Twain

Mark Twain is not Mark Twain. At least he wasn't always.

Though few, if any, remember Samuel Langhorne Clemens. It really doesn't matter anyway.

Of the plethora of American writers who have filled library shelves and enthralled readers throughout the decades, few were as unique as the one who would introduce the world to Tom Sawyer and Huckleberry Finn.

"Twain," of course, means two. It was a reference to his days as a riverboat pilot on the winding Mississippi, which he loved. "Two fathoms deep" meant safe water for a steamboat.

Could this choice of pseudonym be not only a nod to his personal history, but also his approach to his writing? Mark Twain would navigate the depths of society while keeping a certain distance, using humor and satire along the way.

According to Ron Powers, it marked Clemens' transformation from a journeyman printer and sometime journalist to a literary celebrity.*

Southern Roots

Clemens' early life was immersed in the unique rhythms and life of the American South in the early 1800s. It was a world of stark contrast. While the sprawling plantations and rolling riverbanks offered a picturesque view, the nation was still embroiled in the grim reality of slavery

Hannibal, Missouri, where Clemens would spend his formative years, became a setting for Twain's most famous writings. According to Terrell Dempsey, it was also a microcosm of the antebellum South, where the institution of slavery existed alongside the romantic ideals of small-town life. This contradiction would deeply influence Twain's later social criticism.**

While the painted fences and manicured lawns were lined against town streets where ladies in fine dresses walked, slavery cast a long shadow over the landscape. People were nothing more than commodities to be bought and sold at a market.

This cruel treatment of fellow humans was on full display.

Young Sam witnessed this, and on a daily basis, though his family also owned slaves. In fact, the family's servant, Jenny, along with others, would be inspiration for the standout character Jim in Huckleberry Finn.***

It was these exposures, not the idyllic lifestyles of the rich and important, that would leave a fixed mark and forever

---

* Powers, Ron, *Mark Twain: A Life* (Free Press, 2005), 79.

** Dempsey, Terrell, *Searching for Jim: Slavery in Sam Clemens's World* (University of Missouri Press, 2003), 42.

*** Fishkin, Shelley Fisher, *Was Huck Black?: Mark Twain and African-American Voices* (Oxford University Press, 1993), 85.

shape his writings as Mark Twain. Samuel Clemens would grow up viewing and understanding the reality of social and moral contradictions.

How could a society that purported itself to be polite and refined be so cruel to those they considered not fully human? This must have seemed absurd to Clemens and would form a growing narrative to be expressed in the pages of fiction that mirrored, and perhaps impacted, real life in the American South.

A Different Kind of Schooling

Clemens' education, like many children's in that era, could be considered a bit piecemeal. While there was formal schooling, more of a student's education would be from experience and simply observing real life.

Formal teaching took place in the typical one-room schoolhouse with its hard benches and strict rules and learning by rote. But Twain's more tangible learning came from both the streets and the river, where he would engage and learn from steamboat men, entertainers, and storytellers on porches or in local stores.

The Art of Storytelling

The oral tradition of passing down stories is as old as man's ability to speak.

Consider the flavor of this art saturated with the expressions of the South. One fact is clear: the tales, which would often grow larger with each telling, would greatly influence Twain's own ability to tell his story.

Young Sam Clemens absorbed the rhythms and techniques of oral storytelling from both Black and white storytellers in Hannibal. His earliest education in narrative came from listening to slave stories on his uncle's farm and from the tale-telling gatherings at the local general stores and printing offices.*

He would adapt the value of the well-timed pause, the art of humorous exaggeration, and the ability to string together words that would form the sardonic phrases for which he would become known, loved, and hated.

Answering the Call

Any war can affect a person, or people, in many different ways, but everyone is affected just the same. They could either escape and seek to find themselves far removed from the direct bearing the bloody conflict between the states would bring or take up arms.

For others that was impossible, as it was for American society and the nation as a whole. The Civil War affected everything from the economic to the political, and, of course, the personal. The soldiers who decided to join the fight, and were fortunate enough to survive, would not leave their final battlefield the same way they entered.

Samuel Clemens was one of those who joined the fight, though it was short lived. It was the Confederate Militia in the year 1862.

It lasted two weeks.

In his own words, Twain described it this way:

"I had been honestly and sincerely a Confederate rebel; but, as I laid the matter out in that brief campaign, I was converted— not by the enemy's arguments, or my personal observation of the enemy, for I saw none of either—but by being on the losing side. That was enough for me." **

---

* Zall, Paul M., *Mark Twain Laughing: Humorous Anecdotes by and About Samuel L. Clemens* (University of Tennessee Press, 1985), 23.

** Twain, Mark, "The Private History of a Campaign That Failed," *Century Magazine*, December 1885.

While this quote has a mix of humor and fatality, or at least a sense of futility, it's an expression of disillusionment. The reality of war had dashed young Twain's enthusiasm and reshaped his perspective of a cause he now viewed as one destined to fail.

This experience would not be totally wasted as it would be loosely reflected upon in a partially fictional story titled *The Private History of a Campaign That Failed*. In it, Twain would make light of his brief and disappointing time in the militia.

There were those who romanticized the war. Twain's cold critique was an attempt to counter that type of view.

Twain's ability to honestly assess and express opinions that were often contrary to popular views of the day would become a hallmark in his writing and commentary.

Against the Grain

Worthy writing mixes both substance and style for the greatest possible effect. Mark Twain's contained each, along with another key element: *aim*.

The hallmark of his often contrarian thoughts and words was in challenging the social and cultural norms of the times, though the basic truths still live on in many situations today.

As William Faulkner put it, in a day when politicians, preachers, and pedagogues were busy hanging garlands around everything American like so many Christmas-tree decorations, Twain had the bravery to look at the holler places and say what many were afraid to think.[***]

This, of course, does not happen in a vacuum or by default. Writing is creation from the spirit and essence of one's own life. Mark Twain was no exception. In imagining enduring characters with the last names Sawyer and Finn, he would also find and fashion his voice.

[***] William Faulkner, *The Sound and the Fury* (Vintage Books, 1990), 120.

His was a distinctively American one. Some would say it was born out of genius.

He likely would have as well.

Writing is creation from the spirit
and essence of one's own life.

A Frog and a Leap Forward

Perhaps dissecting (no put intended) his first breakout story about a "jumping frog" could provide an inside look into the elements of Twain's colorful and inventive writing.

Set during the Gold Rush, "The Celebrated Jumping Frog of Calaveras County" tells the tale of a man named Jim Smiley who clearly had a propensity to gamble. In fact, he would gamble on just about anything involving any animal, horse, dog, cat, or even chicken, if he believed he would win.

As to not retell the entire story and cause Mark Twain's faithful readers any angst, the hero of this saga, the toad named Dan'l Webster, who was purported to be the fastest jumper in Calaveras County, was done in by the same kind of fraud that was often laid on Jim Smiley. A gullet full of quail shot does not a fast frog make.

Readers of this short story were likely delighted by Twain's sense of humor and language, as well as his keen observation of the societal nuances of the times. If analyzed, this first foray onto the national literary stage offers several key characteristics of Twain's writing that would live with him throughout his life and career.

The tale's success lay not merely in its humor but in its masterful use of the vernacular frame narrative, a technique that would become one of Twain's signatures. The story represented, as James Cox observed, the first successful fusion of frontier humor with a more sophisticated literary technique.*

"The Celebrated Jumping Frog of Calaveras County" captured the American spirit and would be a first solid footprint in the future, cementing of Mark Twain as a beloved American storyteller.

It certainly would not be his last.

Iconic Twain

Even if one hasn't read *Tom Sawyer* or *The Adventures of Huckleberry Finn*, the average reader can cite who wrote them. These are generally considered Mark Twain's greatest works, though his literary repertoire is vast, including *The Prince and the Pauper*, *A Connecticut Yankee in King Arthur's Court*, and *Life on the Mississippi,* each interlaced with Twain's singular voice and brash social commentary.

---

* Cox, James M., *Mark Twain: The Fate of Humor* (Princeton University Press, 1966), 54.

The best novels do more than simply entertain. They are reflective, either to the reader or community at large. Thus, *The Adventures of Tom Sawyer* (1876) and *Adventures of Huckleberry Finn* (1884) would hold a mirror up to the nation itself, revealing both its potential and its ironies.

Fence Painting and Profit

Captured in an author's portrayal of small-town American life, the famed story of Tom Sawyer and painting the fence demonstrates what could be termed innovative influence.

Initially seen as a punishment, or certainly an unwelcome chore, young Tom would completely flip the situation to his good by enlisting friends who initially teased him about having to work.

"Does a boy get a chance to whitewash a fence every day?" This question seemingly shifts the perspectives of the onlookers to the degree where they actually want to take turns with what they now see as a grand opportunity.

This is reflective of the American dream, which can appear very bright and shiny but isn't quite what it seems. All that glitters isn't gold. However, what it demonstrates in regard to ingenuity is more playful than malicious.

Concerning the work as a whole, it demonstrated the complexity of Twain's patriotism and portrayal of small-town America, with its social, religious, and community trappings. Often, he would criticize as he would celebrate, though love of country would always shine through.

Life with Tom Sawyer would be an honest story and depiction of an America that is both wonderful and flawed but still worthy of pride as well as open scrutiny.

More often than not, Twain would use sharp humor to drive that point home.

Morality and Conscience

As mentioned, Twain lived and wrote during the blight on America that was the Civil War. With Huckleberry Finn, he takes the reader deep into what could be described as a moral wilderness, forcing him or her to grapple with the national transgression of slavery.

How can patriotism exist in the face of such barbaric treatment of fellow human beings? The relationship between Huck and Jim serves as a powerful metaphor for moral leadership and true patriotism. In a moment in which Huck could betray Jim, but instead decides to *"go to hell,"* he is choosing a higher calling over simply conforming to societal norms.

Most likely Twain was expressing that, often, the most patriotic thing one can do is oppose wrongs that the populace has deemed acceptable. This journey is one all would-be patriots must travel, especially those who would lead.

Twain makes it clear that true love of country includes standing up for what's right, not just what is popular, as the two often don't meet. Through the awakening of Huck's moral perception, it becomes clear that taking a stand against a nation's failings and moral inconsistencies invites its better angels and actions.

The Mighty Mississippi and Character

Like many writers, Twain loved metaphors. However, the Mississippi was more than that for this former helmsman. He had much on which to reflect, however, in comparing the famed body of water to the reality of American life. The surface can appear smooth while, at the same time, concealing danger beneath.

This could also often describe the community about which Twain would so colorfully write.

Riverboat pilots must be able to navigate and find guidance, regardless of the challenges. Through his masterworks, Twain suggests that effective leadership and true patriotism share common ground. Both require these characteristics:

★ The courage to see clearly rather than comfortably

★ The wisdom to question received truth

★ The strength to stand against popular opinion when conscience demands

★ The ability to love one's community while acknowledging its flaws

American Paradox: Leadership in a Complex Nation

Calling on his experience and perspective, as a riverboat pilot, Twain saw America much like the mighty Mississippi. It was a nation of stark contrasts. Calm on the surface, churning underneath.

It was both a land of liberty and opportunity and of chains and bondage.

His writing would deftly navigate and slice these waters, showing that patriotism for the country meant both honoring what's best about America while also charting a better course for the future.

Honest leadership will hold these truths and pursuits in perfect tension.

Through Tom's adventures, we see the energy and creativity of American life, but also its tendency toward superficiality and conformity. Through Huck's moral journey, we witness the possibility of growth and change, both personal and national. Together, these works suggest that true love of country isn't about blind praise but about engaged citizenship and moral courage.

The Conscience of the Nation

Whether it was painting fences or floating down the Mississippi River, the characters Mark Twain created showed America, and the world, that it's the path less traveled, not the easy one, that leads to change.

Tom's schemes can point to a deeper truth—that the normal way is not always the right or best way. Huck's decision to choose friendship with Jim over societal beliefs showed courage and the power of love over cultural failings.

Even if that meant standing alone.

Faithful to his name, Mark Twain offered the duality of what it meant to truly love one's country. His famous words that opened this chapter still ring true. While a nation deserves constant devotion, the jury will always be out when it comes to government.

It is run by people, after all. And, thus, imperfect.

Twain made it clear that those who lead America must earn the trust of the same. It must be honest enough to spot and correct the issues that lurk below, that will snag, and potentially wreck any vessel and steer around them.

What perfect wisdom from the riverboat pilot turned sardonic storyteller.

Mark Twain showed America,
and the world, that it's the path less traveled,
not the easy one, that leads to change.

Legacy for Modern Leaders

For contemporary leaders, Twain's masterworks offer crucial insights about navigating complex moral and social territories. They remind us that leadership isn't just about achieving goals but about serving higher purposes. They suggest that patriotism isn't just about flying flags but about fighting for national ideals.

In an era of increasing polarization and moral complexity, Twain's insights into leadership and patriotism remain vitally relevant. His characters show us that effective leaders must balance multiple truths: the need for social cohesion with the importance of moral courage, the value of tradition with the necessity of change, the love of country with the recognition of its flaws.

Quips and Quotes

Twain is remembered for encapsulating his wit and wisdom into memorable phrases, often referred to in today's age as one-liners.

While there could be some that would disparage these kinds of sayings as superficial or flippant, there is typically a valuable truth that can be discovered and applied hidden beneath what the critic would dismiss as an off-handed remark.

Twain's quotes ranged from comedic to cynical, and also inspiring. Reflecting on some of his more enduring comments can serve to shed more light on his view of the world around him and the perspective he wished to share.

"The secret of getting ahead is getting started."

Procrastination and progress don't mix. Nor does perfectionism. There is a time to dream and a time to take that first step toward realization. Then the second and the third.

"The two most important days in your life are the day you are born and the day you find out why."

One of the biggest questions man has to answer surrounds purpose and meaning. Another way of stating this is that everyone is born, but not everyone really lives. Even leaders can fall into the trap of simply existing and drifting through life. But for the great ones, self-discovery and mission are paramount.

"Travel is fatal to prejudice, bigotry, and narrow-mindedness."

This is curious phrasing and use of the word *fatal*. Cleary, the familiar and unaffected paradigm will keep the mind trained on labeling others, or stereotyping, alive and well, though toxic.

Part of why people engage in stereotyping is that it's lazy or easy. Travel is one example of discovering the new, as it relates to people who are different.

Information overcomes assumptions.

"If you tell the truth, you don't have to remember anything."

Honesty unclutters the mind and life. Liars need exceptionally good memories. One has to maintain a list and frame of reference for all the untruths that have been told.

Not only is that stressful, but unnecessarily so.

"Courage is resistance to fear, mastery of fear, not absence of fear."

No one is a stranger to fear. And a healthy fear is necessary.

Fear unbridled can be paralyzing.

Waiting for it to be completely expelled is exasperating. Perhaps part of resisting is determining what fear is reasonable and what is worthy of disregard while moving forward.

David L. Smith notes: *"This definition of courage emerged from Twain's own experiences with fear and conflict. It represents a mature understanding that true bravery isn't fearlessness, but rather the ability to act despite one's fears."*[*]

"It is better to keep your mouth closed and let people think you are a fool than to open it and remove all doubt."

---

[*] Smith, D.L., *Mark Twain's Civil War* (University Press of Kentucky, 1994).

This harkens back to the proverb that conveys that a person can appear wise simply by not speaking.

The alternative often betrays and produces the opposite result.

Sometimes silence is wisdom.

"Age is an issue of mind over matter. If you don't mind, it doesn't matter."

Certainly, only a play on words. Or is it? There can be no question how important state of mind is.

While that won't change the date on one's birth certificate, it can inform how we navigate the aging process.

"The man who does not read has no advantage over the man who cannot read."

Benjamin Franklin dropped out of school when he was ten years old. Many would argue, however, that he became one of the great minds of his day. How? *Reading*.

"Kindness is the language which the deaf can hear and the blind can see."

Again, mastery of wordplay and phrasing. Likely Twain was referencing not only the physical, but also the sociologic inabilities that true compassion can overcome.

Charitable actions can be universal and understood by everyone, regardless of circumstance.

"Never argue with a fool. Onlookers may not be able to tell the difference."

One can almost hear Twain's voice upon reading this. Certainly, his dry, satirical humor bites through. Probably the best advice on arguments is to simply avoid them. How would one know if the other is a fool? Better to avoid the crowd placing that label on both participants inadvertently.

"Actions speak louder than words but not nearly as often."

There are similar quotes that allude to this same truth. "Talk is cheap," for example. Words matter only when they are accompanied by credible action. Otherwise, alignment could be mistaken for laziness or hypocrisy.

The gap between declaration and deed was a constant target of Twain's satire. He recognized that while actions might speak louder than words, human nature tends toward the path of least resistance—talking rather than doing.[*]

"The human race has one really effective weapon, and that is laughter."

Twain understood the disarming and neutralizing impact humor can have on people.

It can ease tension, soothe wounds, and connect people. He would use this "weapon" in many of his writings to reach and bridge audiences with a wide range of social divide.

Leading with Laughter and Scorn

While it would be easy to dismiss the works of Mark Twain as mere entertaining fiction, as well as insight into southern living, his writing goes much deeper.

---

[*] Brodwin, Stanley, *Mark Twain's Humorous Perspective* (Chicago University Press, 1989), 245.

His perspective demonstrates a kind of love for country and a patriotic spirit that was willing to challenge the status quo and bring into question the ills and, often, absurdity, of the world around him.

That's the "two" that Twain often balanced in his storytelling.

The call for social change can come from many different circles and corners, even from a failed private of the Confederate Militia named Samuel Clemens.

Twain may not have considered himself a leader, but he certainly was an agent for change, and his literature still inspires other writers to employ their talent to advocate for progress in society.

He struck a delicate balance between humor and critique, urging readers to embrace what's beautiful about America while honestly and tirelessly working for a more fair and just society.

Mark Twain loved his country, not in a blind way, but reflectively, taking an honest look at the praiseworthy and the scornful, always striving to make it better.

Twain Leadership Principles

★ **Wield Truth with Authority:** Twain used honesty as his sharpest weapon against injustice. Real leaders understand truth's transformative force.

★ **Master the Art of Influence:** Through humor and storytelling, Twain moved hearts and changed minds. Leaders must perfect their tools of persuasion.

★ **Challenge a Comfortable Culture:** Twain confronted society's accepted hypocrisies. True leaders question what others passively accept.

★ **Speak with Authentic Voice:** In an era of flowery language, Twain wrote how people actually talked. Leaders communicate with genuine distinctiveness.

★ **Patriotism Requires Balance:** Twain loved his country enough to criticize its flaws. Real leadership includes the courage to correct what you cherish.

★ **Learn from Every Source:** Twain gained wisdom in many subjects, from riverboats to royal courts. Leaders gather insights from both common and extraordinary experiences.

★ **Lead with Compassionate Understanding:** Through characters like Jim, Twain showed the power of human dignity. True leaders see and uplift humanity in everyone.

Chapter Nine

Harriet Tubman – American Crusader

"If you hear the dogs, keep going. If you see the torches in the woods, keep going. If there's shouting after you, keep going. Don't ever stop. Keep going. If you want a taste of freedom, keep going."

—Harriet Tubman

If ever there is a permanent stain on the history of America, it is slavery.

The owning of a human being by another, while not exclusive to the United States, was abhorrent, cruel, and simply wrong. It robbed people of the basic freedoms many today take for granted, treating them as property rather than actual individuals.

It removed their sense of dignity and self-worth and subjected them to the worst kinds of brutality and abuse, including physical, psychological, and verbal. Slavery separated families, tearing children from parents and siblings, husbands from wives, mothers from daughters, fathers from sons.

Slavery fueled and perpetuated the worst kinds of ideology linked to prejudice and discrimination, leading to a degradation of a would-be united nation. It fostered economic exploitation for the sake of expediency and free labor.

Slaves remained poor while bosses and owners got rich.

It struck and pierced the heart of any and all moral and Godly principles for which American was founded in the first place.

In short, slavery was sin.

It became America's enduring transgression. A dark legacy that still echoes today.

Thankfully, not every corner of the nation supported the base practice of enslavement. There certainly was opposition from varied sources. There were also differing degrees. As with any all-encompassing issue such as slavery, individuals, communities, and government entities decided how active, loud, or quiet they wished to be in dissenting against something so prevailing to be a national divide.

Some supported abolition, swift and complete. Others suggested a more gradual solution. It was likely the total of similar efforts, not to mention the 13th Amendment, which would all play a role in the eventual eradication of slavery in America.

One can only wonder how many witnessed or were directly, or indirectly, affected by slavery and remained silent or passive. Could such apathy have furthered the damaging cycle of human exploitation?

It would be hard to argue otherwise.

While there were those who distinguished themselves as dissenters and activists against slavery, such as Frederick Douglas, William Garrison, John Brown, and many others, few marked themselves in such a daring and unique way as Harriet Tubman.

Her life represents the plight and angst of every person born a slave: the desire and fight to be free. Tubman would realize this freedom, through harrowing circumstances, for herself and eventually numerous others.

Beginning in Bondage

Her story, though, began as typical of countless other Black people in America, *in captivity*. As a result, as it was for all born into slavery, her early life was ravaged by hardship and ruthlessness.

Originally known as Araminta Ross, she would later borrow her mother's first name, Harriet. As a young girl, though, she was "hired out" to many different owners, facing a shifting degree of bitter treatment and beatings. One such incident, which involved a heavy metal weight, caused a severe head injury.

This would lead to headaches and narcolepsy for the rest of her life.

The severe head trauma Tubman suffered as a young woman, while horrific, may have contributed to her powerful spiritual visions that she later credited as divine guidance for her rescue missions.*

---

* Sernett, Milton C., *Harriet Tubman: Myth, Memory, and History* (Duke University Press, 2007), p. 25.

Even so, hints of her leadership qualities and empathetic nature were evident, as she grounded her life in faith and the belief in the equality of *all* people.

What an ironic internal perspective from one facing such an oppressive outward reality. Legacy leadership always has germinations in the heart. Tubman's early life is a crucial example of *character* over *circumstances*.

Though it wasn't just valuable traits and characteristics being developed that would be key later in life, but essential skills. Her father would teach her how to navigate through the woods and the swamp, experience and training that would serve her well when it came time to help others do the same.

Fearing that she would be sold and separated from her family, she made a courageous and death-defying decision to escape. The North Star would lead her along, with the aid of the Underground Railroad, to her eventual destination.

To freedom.

According to Kate Clifford Larson's definitive biography, Harriet Tubman escaped in September 1849 when she was around twenty-seven years old.*

The decision to escape was precipitated by her fear of being sold further south after her owner, Edward Brodess, died in March 1849, leaving his widow Mary in financial difficulty. This fear intensified when she learned that two of her sisters, Mary and Linah, had been sold to a slave trader headed for the Deep South.**

This was a ninety-mile trek.

Consider that aspect alone. On foot, and through varied terrain, that much distance would be a challenge for any

---

* Larson, Kate Clifford, *Bound for the Promised Land: Harriet Tubman, Portrait of an American Hero* (Ballantine Books, 2004), 80.

** Clinton, Catherine, *Harriet Tubman: The Road to Freedom* (Little, Brown and Company, 2004), 31.

traveler. This was no ordinary journey. For the slave attempting to steal freedom, these attempts were fraught with persistent peril. Looking over one's shoulder was a given.

Leaving on a Saturday, under the cover of darkness, her hope was that her absence would not be noticed until Monday. In her mind, this was a head start.

Once she reached the state of Pennsylvania, victory was close at hand. But she could not fully relax until reaching Philadelphia, a stronghold for abolitionists and where many central network operators could be found. The birthplace of American freedom had become a haven for many still fighting for those ideals on behalf of countless others who were not afforded them at that time.

Inspired by a Freer World

While America as a whole was still enveloped in slavery, Tubman's initial entrance into Philadelphia must have been quite the revelation. She would have been quick to perceive that life in general was much different than what she experienced in Maryland, given that the city was currently a cluster for abolitionist activity and its agents. This would include organizations like the Pennsylvania Abolition Society who aided fugitive slaves.

William Still would have been an early contact, but not her last. Still was key, however, as he was one of the more prominent Black abolitionists with another group, the Philadelphia Vigilance Committee, who also helped runaway slaves and kept records of those passing through the city.

At the height of all these connections and early encounters, Tubman got a taste of what it was like to be free for the first time in her life.

To say this was inspiring would likely have been an understatement. She was very probably thrilled by the prospect of what she witnessed and could already be thinking of others who needed to share in this new reality. These stirrings would prove to be a pivotal moment in both her life and the history of the Underground Railroad, as they would eventually coincide in dramatic fashion.

Legacy leadership always has
germinations in the heart.

Catalytic flashes occur when awareness of a need joins with what one can uniquely do to meet it.

Run to the Rescue

What would the average person do when they found freedom after a life of slavery and cruelty? A reasonable conclusion would be that once experienced, the taste of liberation would be something not only cherished, but not to be relinquished.

Picture entering a world where, despite your skin color or place of origin, you could seek to obtain a life disparate from the one you just moments ago were trapped in, reduced to under the shackles of slavery.

There was hope that you might be, and be perceived as, a man or woman with the kind of dignity that should be afforded *any* human being. This hope was strong enough to leave behind the years of torment and begin to discern the goodness that true freedom might bring.

How could anyone feel that and ever want to let it go?

Yet there was something in Harriet Tubman's heart that would pull her thoughts back. She remembered others who should receive this healing balm of liberty.

She famously said, *"I was free, and they should be free."*

Who were "they"? Who were those Harriet knew were still behind, in Dorchester County, and neighboring areas on Maryland's Eastern Shore, but never far from her mind?

- **Her siblings**: Several brothers and sisters of Tubman were still enslaved. Brothers Ben, Henry, and Robert and sister Rachel were high on the list of family members to be liberated, if possible.

- **Her parents**: Harriet "Rit" Green was also still enslaved at the time of her first escape. Even though her father, Ben Ross, had legally been freed in 1840, he stayed close to his wife and children who did not enjoy the same circumstance.

- **Her husband**: At the time of her escape, Tubman had a husband named John Tubman, who was a free Black man. He did not agree with the idea of leaving Maryland and thus did not join her when she took flight.

   In an unrelenting effort, Harriet would later return to have him join her once again, but by then, he had remarried.

- **Her nieces and nephews**: Tubman was exceptionally troubled regarding the children of her siblings.

- **Others**: Beyond her immediate family, Tubman felt a responsibility to help other enslaved people she knew from the community where she had previously been held in captivity.

Imagine the emotions and reflections that had to be engulfing her psyche. Emotions can guide, nudge, and often rule the mind. Every leader knows that. Every human being should.

Again, balancing the newly found freedom and elation Tubman must have felt with the overarching sense of obligation towards those still in captivity must have been an immense dichotomy indeed.

While it's impossible to say all the exact feelings Tubman was processing, some reasonable inference can be made based on her own accounting.

Fear

Far removed from this period in our nation's history, it can be difficult to comprehend fully the enormous risks and dangers for a freed person *returning* to slave territory.

As historian Kate Clifford Larson notes:

> The dangers Tubman faced were extraordinary. The Eastern Shore counties had established heavily armed patrols specifically targeting suspected Underground Railroad operators. A return journey meant risking not just re-enslavement, but likely execution.*

Remember, fear can be, and often is, a paralyzing emotion. Of course, there's healthy fear. It could be argued that this qualified here. To revisit where you were once a slave in an attempt to free others still captive was certainly not reasonable.

Despite the trepidation that may have been coursing through her veins, Harriet still chose to act.

Empathy

Who better to understand the plight of those still enslaved than one recently liberated from that awful plight? Many in America at the time wanted to, and even did, sympathize with slaves, but could they actually *empathize*?

No. These are two different emotional responses to the difficulties of others. Almost anyone, with even a moderate level of compassion, can say they feel sorry for someone in trouble.

---

* Larson, Kate Clifford, *Bound for the Promised Land: Harriet Tubman, Portrait of an American Hero* (Ballantine Books, 2004), 115.

That's sympathy. *Empathy* involves truly desiring to understand how one undergoes that situation. Often it is because they have a shared experience.

It's easy to surmise that Harriet Tubman could still "feel" the sting of the oppressive tools used to intimidate those in bondage.

She could likely picture faces and hear their voices, whether she wanted to or not. She bore scars and permanent wounds, both physical and otherwise, inflicted by these traumatic events and the cruelty of others.

Tubman could empathize with current slaves because it was only by the grace of God and a short passage of time that she wasn't still walking in those very same shoes.

No one is greatly moved by mere sympathy. Empathy usually precedes stronger, more impactful, and lasting deeds.

Guilt

Selfish people typically do not feel guilt over enjoying something others haven't or may never experience. Only selfless individuals grapple with such emotions and may question why they receive goodness that someone else didn't.

History tells us which kind of person and leader Harriet Tubman was. It's possible those thoughts and feelings were with her even during her treacherous first journey to Philadelphia.

Modern historian Milton C. Sernett analyzes this aspect of Tubman's motivation: "What we might today recognize as 'survivor's guilt' played a significant role in Tubman's decision to return. Her initial freedom felt incomplete while her family remained enslaved."**

** Sernett, Milton C., *Harriet Tubman: Myth, Memory, and History* (Duke University Press, 2007), 182.

The wide gulf, no doubt, felt more distant knowing that her family members were still forced to endure the hellish life she was able to flee.

Anger

If there was no other emotion present for Harriet Tubman, perhaps this one would have been enough. Anger can be destructive, but it can also be righteous and justified. Many were enraged, not to mention deeply divided—violently so—regarding slavery.

It was evident on the battlefield, in the newspapers, and in political circles, and it would eventually lead to a presidential assassination. For Tubman, the pure inequality of slavery, the owning of other human beings, was fuel for the most virtuous rage that would lead to not only the rescue of others but acts against the system itself.

This was anger justified.

Emotions can guide, nudge,
and often rule the mind.

Religious Conviction

While not actually an emotion, faith in God certainly can be a driving force in summoning vast amounts of courage and moral indignation for a worthy cause. Tubman must have believed this was part of her divine purpose and, as such, believed she was not only prompted by God but protected by Him as well.

It's feasible to conclude that Tubman believed in something, or Someone, more powerful than she, more awesome than the monstrosity that was slavery. She believed herself called to risk her life to run to the rescue for the sake of others.

Emotions can be powerful, even primal, but often are superfluous or not necessarily attached to deep issues. The horror of slavery was not a small matter by any means.

While only Tubman knows which, or all, of these had an impact on her decision to return and save those left behind, ultimately history says that she did.

And this, more than once.

In her own testimony to Sarah Bradford, Tubman explained: *"I always told God, 'I'm going to hold steady on to you, and you've got to see me through.'"* *

Emotions alone are not enough to succeed in something as daring as what Tubman pursued, though quite potent when matched with planning and proper resources.

A Path That Preceded

While some may believe, incorrectly, that Harriet Tubman started the Underground Railroad, that's an extra part of her story that is more legend than truth. This network of people, houses, and secret routes started in the late eighteenth century and had its peak between 1850 and 1860.

While Harriet Tubman did not found this key resource for those escaping slavery, she would become one of its most skilled and celebrated "conductors."

Eric Foner takes it a step further. The Underground Railroad, with Tubman as one of its most effective conductors, represented America's first interracial civil rights movement, bringing together Black and white abolitionists in a common cause.**

---

* Bradford, Sarah H., *Scenes in the Life of Harriet Tubman* (W.J. Moses, 1869), 48.

** Foner, Eric, *Gateway to Freedom: The Hidden History of the Underground Railroad* (Norton, 2015), 115.

Her first trip, following her own journey to freedom, was for her niece and her children.

Consider how paramount and pivotal this was in the life of a former slave. Once the decision was made, action must follow. In this case, the most daring kind. What if this mission had failed in some way or she had not completed that initial trek back to Maryland and slave territory? It can be easily surmised that the goal, the prize of family freed from captivity, would not allow her mission to be thwarted.

One can easily surmise it was this all-in, ongoing mission that would prompt the woman who would become known to her people as "Moses" to, in her own words, "keep going."

Unsung Heroes of the Underground Railroad

Because many had to operate in secret, not all the names of those connected to the Underground Railroad are known. Suffice it to say, Harriet Tubman did not act alone in her life-saving work. It could be easy to view this dynamic and successful liberator as almost superhuman.

No. All legends are still mere mortals. Ordinary people who could rise above the mundane and achieve the extraordinary.

But not without help.

"If you want to go fast, go alone. If you want to go far, go together."
—African proverb

Harriet Tubman was wise enough to know that longevity was more important than speed, though the latter was gravely important as well.

As mentioned earlier in this chapter, the willing who were a crucial part of the network that constituted the Underground Railroad, and similar efforts, were of no small note. Even someone as celebrated as Frederick Douglas offered his home as a station for the railroad.

Some Native American communities would assist slaves, especially in the north, to continue that trek towards freedom. Quakers were staunch abolitionists and would aid the railroad. Black communities that were free would assist with shelter and food.

Every leader should know he or she can't reach great heights alone. That only happens in the mind of an egotist.

For Harriet Tubman, the mission was the hero of the story. It was for each soul to be brought out of bondage and into what had to be described as the promised land.

All legends are still mere mortals. Ordinary people who could rise above the mundane and achieve the extraordinary.

Moral Leadership in Action

Not everyone in 1860s America believed slavery was wrong. Given that the history of owning people began long before, so then did the seeds that would eventually take root.

The result was a country divided between those who saw slavery as a necessary evil and others who knew it was fundamentally abhorrent.

Even the founders wrestled with this, including compromises as an insufficient way to resolve the issue. Thomas Jefferson forcefully condemned slavery in his initial draft of the Declaration of Independence, yet he remained one of Virginia's largest slave owners until his death.*

Controversy exists when opinion trumps truth and compassion. What one thinks is right can lead to more contemplation, further discussion, perhaps growth, or something more dramatic.

---

* Jefferson, Thomas, *Notes on the State of Virginia* (First published privately, 1785).

Even heroic.

For Harriet Tubman, her sense of right and justice for those oppressed prompted her to risk her life so that others could receive and enjoy the kind of freedom she was able to steal.

To say that Tubman was a leader is a given. Listing her as a patriotic leader is more fitting.

Like Lincoln, her influence, per her station in life, arrived at a time of extreme and violent divide in a still relatively young America.

She had no easy road on which to travel, figurative or otherwise. What she was able to accomplish, not just with her work with the Underground Railroad, but beyond, presents an example of the enduring value of lifting others.

During the Civil War, Tubman operated as a spy and a nurse for the Union Army, even leading an armed expedition that freed over 700 people.

She was the first woman to do so.

She would also go on to fight for women's right to vote.

Upon her deathbed, she quoted Jesus' words, *"I go to prepare a place for you."* (John 14:2)

Fitting for one who, placing herself in harm's way, saved so many and helped them obtain their place in a freer world.

Tubman's Leadership Principles

★ **Turn Fear into Fuel:** Tubman converted mortal danger into determined action. Real leaders channel fear into purposeful strength.

★ **Lead from Moral Conviction:** Tubman's unwavering sense of right drove her to extraordinary deeds. Leaders must be anchored in unshakeable principles.

★ **Take Direct Action:** While others debated slavery, Tubman personally rescued dozens. True leaders move beyond words to decisive action.

★ **Leave No One Behind:** Despite achieving her own freedom, Tubman repeatedly risked everything for others. Real leadership demands personal sacrifice for the greater good.

★ **Navigate Through Darkness:** Tubman mastered both physical and metaphorical obstacles. Leaders find ways forward when others see no path.

★ **Build Networks of Trust:** Tubman's success depended on a carefully cultivated web of allies. Leaders create and nurture connections that enable greater impact.

★ **Inspire Through Example:** Tubman's courage motivated others to join her cause. True leaders inspire not through words alone, but through demonstrated conviction.

Epilogue

Extending the Legacy: More Leaders Who Defined a Nation

As the lives of nine remarkable individuals have been highlighted and chronicled, time and history will not let us forget the many other patriots whose stories have been added to the story of America. It is fitting to also acknowledge the vision, bravery, and commitment that has left an indelible mark on the national narrative.

Here are their names and brief profiles:

★ **George Washington**: Patriarch and the first president of the United States, known for his exceptional leadership during the American Revolution as well as his pivotal role in forming a new nation.

★ **Thomas Jefferson**: Author of the Declaration of Independence and the third president of the United States whose vision of democracy continues to influence American ideals.

- ★ **Alexander Hamilton**: A Founding Father and the first secretary of the treasury whose financial policies helped establish the economic foundation of the United States.

- ★ **John Adams**: A Founding Father and the second president of the United States, who played a key role in advocating for independence.

- ★ **Thomas Paine:** Influential writer and revolutionary whose pamphlet "Common Sense" inspired American independence and democratic ideals.

- ★ **Benjamin Franklin**: A polymath and Founding Father whose contributions to science, diplomacy, and politics were pivotal in the formation of the United States.

- ★ **Abraham Lincoln:** The sixteenth president of the United States, who led the country through the Civil War and worked to end slavery with the Emancipation Proclamation.

- ★ **Dwight D. Eisenhower:** Supreme Allied Commander during World War II and the thirty-fourth president of the United States, who led the nation through significant post-war change.

- ★ **John F. Kennedy:** The thirty-fifth president of the United States, known for his inspirational leadership during the Civil Rights Movement and the Space Race.

- ★ **Franklin D. Roosevelt:** The thirty-second President of the United States, who led the country through the Great Depression and World War II.

- ★ **Susan B. Anthony**: A pioneering advocate for women's rights, whose tireless efforts were instrumental in securing women's suffrage.

★ **Frederick Douglass**: An eloquent abolitionist and former enslaved person, who fought for the abolition of slavery and the rights of African Americans.

★ **Rosa Parks**: A civil rights activist whose refusal to give up her seat on a bus sparked the Montgomery Bus Boycott and advanced the cause of racial equality.

★ **Martin Luther King Jr.**: A visionary leader of the Civil Rights Movement, whose advocacy for nonviolent resistance and equality profoundly changed American society.

★ **Eleanor Roosevelt**: First Lady, diplomat, and activist, who championed human rights and worked tirelessly to improve the lives of the disadvantaged.

★ **Thurgood Marshall**: The first African American Supreme Court justice, whose legal work helped dismantle racial segregation in the United States.

★ **Barbara Jordan:** Lawyer, educator, and politician who was a leader in the Civil Rights Movement and the first African American woman elected to the Texas Senate.

★ **Betsy Ross**: Credited with sewing the first American flag, symbolizing the birth of the nation and its struggle for independence.

★ **Helen Keller**: Activist and author who overcame blindness and deafness to advocate for people with disabilities and women's rights.

★ **Clara Barton**: Founder of the American Red Cross, known for her humanitarian efforts and providing medical care during the Civil War.

★ **Cesar Chavez**: Labor leader and civil rights activist who co-founded the United Farm Workers, advocating for better working conditions and rights for farm workers.

★ **Sojourner Truth**: Abolitionist and women's rights activist who delivered powerful speeches advocating for equality and justice.

★ **Maya Angelou**: Renowned poet, memoirist, and civil rights activist.

★ **Alexander Graham Bell**: Inventor of the telephone whose innovations revolutionized communication.

★ **Jackie Robinson**: The first African American to play Major League Baseball in the modern era, breaking the color barrier and advancing civil rights.

★ **Eli Whitney**: Inventor of the cotton gin, whose creation revolutionized the agricultural industry.

★ **Walt Disney**: Pioneer of the American animation industry, whose creativity and innovation have left a lasting cultural legacy.

★ **Sally Ride**: The first American woman in space, inspiring countless young women to pursue careers in science and engineering.

★ **Jane Addams**: Social reformer and founder of Hull House, who worked to improve the lives of the poor and advocate for women's rights.

★ **Andrew Carnegie**: Industrialist and philanthropist who made significant contributions to the expansion of the American steel industry and donated much of his wealth to public causes.

★ **John Glenn**: Astronaut and the first American to orbit the Earth, symbolizing American pioneering spirit and exploration.

★ **Steve Jobs**: Co-founder of Apple Inc., known for revolutionizing personal technology with the Apple II, Macintosh, iPhone, and other products.

★ **Norman Rockwell**: Renowned artist and illustrator whose works depicted American culture and values, capturing the spirit of everyday life.

★ **Fred Rogers**: Beloved television host of *Mister Rogers' Neighborhood*, known for his gentle and profound influence on children's education and emotional well-being.

★ **Douglas MacArthur**: Prominent military leader whose service in World War II and the Korean War was instrumental in shaping American military strategy and global presence.

★ **Marian Anderson**: Celebrated singer whose performance at the Lincoln Memorial broke racial barriers and inspired the Civil Rights Movement.

★ **Frances Perkins**: The first female member of the U.S. Cabinet, serving as secretary of labor and playing a key role in shaping New Deal policies.

★ **John Muir**: Naturalist and environmental philosopher who advocated for the preservation of wilderness in the United States, founding the Sierra Club.

★ **Henry David Thoreau**: Philosopher, author, and naturalist whose writings on civil disobedience and simple living influenced American thought and social movements.

★ **Jimmy Stewart**: Iconic actor and World War II veteran, known for his enduring performances in classic American films like *It's a Wonderful Life* and *Mr. Smith Goes to Washington,* as well as his service to his country.

★ **Sandra Day O'Connor**: The first woman to serve on the U.S. Supreme Court, known for her pragmatic approach to justice and her influence on American law.

★ **Booker T. Washington**: Influential educator, author, and advisor to several presidents, who played a key role in promoting education and economic self-reliance among African Americans.

★ **James Madison**: Fourth president of the United States and "Father of the Constitution," who played a pivotal role in drafting and promoting the U.S. Constitution and Bill of Rights.

★ **Dolley Madison**: First Lady known for her role in saving important artifacts during the War of 1812 and for her influence in shaping the role of First Lady.

★ **Robert E. Lee**: Renowned Confederate general whose military strategies are studied to this day, despite the controversies surrounding his role in the Civil War.

★ **Clint Eastwood**: Acclaimed actor, director, and cultural icon who has shaped American cinema and portrayed rugged American individualism.

★ **Ruth Bader Ginsburg**: Supreme Court Justice known for her advocacy for gender equality and her influential judicial opinions.

★ **Henry Clay**: Influential statesman and orator known as the "Great Compromiser" for his efforts in navigating the nation through sectional conflicts.

★ **Jonas Salk**: Medical researcher who developed the first successful polio vaccine.

★ **Harriet Beecher Stowe**: Author of *Uncle Tom's Cabin*, which galvanized the abolitionist movement and brought attention to the horrors of slavery.

Bibliography

Books

Adams, Ramon F. *The Old-Time Cowboy*. Norman: University of Oklahoma Press, 1961.

Blumenson, Martin. *The Patton Papers: 1885-1940*. Boston: Houghton Mifflin, 1972.

Blumenson, Martin. *Patton: The Man Behind the Legend*. New York: William Morrow, 1985.

Bradford, Sarah H. *Scenes in the Life of Harriet Tubman*. Auburn: W.J. Moses, 1869.

Bradford, Sarah H. *Harriet Tubman: The Moses of Her People*. New York: Geo. R. Lockwood & Son, 1886.

Bradley, Omar N. *A Soldier's Story*. Henry Holt and Company, 1951.

Brodwin, Stanley. *Mark Twain's Humorous Perspective*. Chicago: University of Chicago Press, 1989.

Brown, Richard D. *Revolutionary Politics in Massachusetts: The Boston Committee of Correspondence and the Towns, 1772-1774*. Cambridge: Harvard University Press, 1970.

Butler, Susan. *East to the Dawn: The Life of Amelia Earhart*. New York: Da Capo Press, 2009.

171

Casey, Robert. *The Model T: A Centennial History.* Baltimore: Johns Hopkins University Press, 2008.

Clinton, Catherine. *Harriet Tubman: The Road to Freedom.* New York: Little, Brown and Company, 2004.

Cochrane, Dorothy. *Pioneers of Flight: Women in Early Aviation.* Washington, D.C.: Smithsonian Press, 2018.

Corn, Joseph J. *The Winged Gospel: America's Romance with Aviation.* Baltimore: Johns Hopkins University Press, 2002.

Cox, James M. *Mark Twain: The Fate of Humor.* Princeton: Princeton University Press, 1966.

Cox, James M. *Mark Twain: The Life.* New York: Public Affairs, 2010.

Davis, Seth. *When March Went Mad: The Game That Transformed Basketball.* New York: Times Books, 2009.

Dempsey, Terrell. *Searching for Jim: Slavery in Sam Clemens's World.* Columbia: University of Missouri Press, 2003.

D'Este, Carlo. *Patton: A Genius for War.* New York: Harper Collins, 1995.

Eisenhower, John S.D. *Intervention!: The United States and the Mexican Revolution, 1913-1917.* New York: W.W. Norton, 1993.

Fishkin, Shelley Fisher. *Was Huck Black?: Mark Twain and African-American Voices.* New York: Oxford University Press, 1993.

Foner, Eric. *Gateway to Freedom: The Hidden History of the Underground Railroad.* New York: Norton, 2015.

Ford, Henry. *My Life and Work: An Autobiography of Henry Ford.* Garden City: Garden City Publishing, 1922.

Hirshson, Stanley P. *General Patton: A Soldier's Life.* New York: Harper Collins, 2002.

Jefferson, Thomas. *Notes on the State of Virginia.* Paris: First published privately, 1785.

Jonas, Manfred. *Isolationism in America, 1935-1941.* Ithaca: Cornell University Press, 1966.

Kouzes, James M., and Barry Z. Posner. *The Leadership Challenge: How to Make Extraordinary Things Happen in Organizations.* 6th ed. Hoboken: John Wiley & Sons, 2017.

Labaree, Benjamin Woods. *The Boston Tea Party.* Boston: Northeastern University Press, 1979.

Larson, Kate Clifford. *Bound for the Promised Land: Harriet Tubman, Portrait of an American Hero.* New York: Ballantine Books, 2004.

Lazenby, Roland. *Michael Jordan: The Life.* New York: Little, Brown and Company, 2014.

Lazenby, Roland. *Michael Jordan: The Rules of Success.* New York: Random House, 2001.

Long, Elgen M. and Marie K. Long. *Amelia Earhart: The Mystery Solved.* New York: Simon & Schuster, 2000.

Maier, Pauline. *From Resistance to Revolution: Colonial Radicals and the Development of American Opposition to Britain, 1765-1776.* New York: Norton, 1991.

Meilinger, Phillip S. *American Military Culture and Strategy.* Military Review, 2007.

Middlekauff, Robert. *The Glorious Cause: The American Revolution, 1763-1789.* New York: Oxford University Press, 2005.

Miller, Mark. *The Birth of Modern America: A History, 1619-1939.* Malden: Blackwell Publishing, 2006.

Morris, Edmund. *The Rise of Theodore Roosevelt.* New York: Coward, McCann & Geoghegan, 1979.

Morris, Edmund. *Theodore Rex.* New York: Random House, 2001.

Nevins, Allan. *Ford: The Times, The Man, The Company.* New York: Charles Scribner's Sons, 1954.

Nye, Roger H. *The Patton Mind: The Professional Development of an Extraordinary Leader.* Garden City Park: Avery Publishing Group, 1993.

O'Connor, Thomas H. *The Hub: Boston Past and Present.* Boston: Northeastern University Press, 2001.

O'Neil, Paul. "The Western Code in Film: From Silver Screen to American Values." *Film History Quarterly*, 1978.

Pershing, John J. *My Experiences in the World War.* Vol. 1. New York: Frederick A. Stokes, 1931.

Phillips, Gervase. "The Saber During the American Civil War and After." *American Military History Journal*, 2001.

Porter, David L. *Michael Jordan: A Biography.* Westport: Greenwood Press, 2007.

Powers, Ron. *Mark Twain: A Life.* New York: Free Press, 2005.

Province, Charles M. *The Unknown Patton.* New York: Hippocrene Books, 1983.

Rae, J. B. "Henry Ford's Contribution to Society." *Journal of Social Progress*, vol. 10, no. 2, 1925, pp. 85-102.

Rich, Doris L. *Amelia Earhart: A Biography.* Washington, D.C.: Smithsonian Institution Press, 1989.

Roosevelt, Theodore. *An Autobiography.* New York: Charles Scribner's Sons, 1913.

Sernett, Milton C. *Harriet Tubman: Myth, Memory, and History.* Durham: Duke University Press, 2007.

Smith, Dean. *A Coach's Life: My Forty Years in College Basketball.* New York: Random House, 2002.

Smith, D.L. *Mark Twain's Civil War.* Lexington: University Press of Kentucky, 1994.

Snow, Richard. *I Invented the Modern Age: The Rise of Henry Ford.* New York: Scribner, 2013.

Sorensen, Charles E. *My Forty Years with Ford.* New York: Norton, 1956.

Stoll, Ira. *Samuel Adams: A Life.* New York: Free Press, 2008.

Unruh Jr., John D. *The Plains Across: The Overland Emigrants and the Trans-Mississippi West, 1840-60.* Urbana: University of Illinois Press, 1979.

Watts, Steven. *The People's Tycoon: Henry Ford and the American Century.* New York: Vintage Books, 2006.

White, Richard. *It's Your Misfortune and None of My Own: A New History of the American West.* Norman: University of Oklahoma Press, 1991.

Wills, Garry. *John Wayne's America: The Politics of Celebrity.* New York: Simon & Schuster, 1997.

Articles and Other Sources

www.brittanica.com

Faulkner, William. *The Sound and the Fury.* New York: Vintage Books, 1990.

"Gallup Poll on American Patriotism." Gallup, accessed February 6, 2025, www.gallup.com.

Harvard University Presidential Papers. "Theodore Roosevelt Address to Harvard University, 1901." Library of Congress.

"History of Samuel Adams." History.com, accessed February 6, 2025, www.history.com.

Loeb, William Jr. "Personal Memories of Theodore Roosevelt." Unpublished manuscript, 1922. Theodore Roosevelt Collection, Harvard University Library.

Maslow, Abraham H. "A Theory of Human Motivation." *Psychological Review* 50, no. 4 (1943): 370-396.

Otis, James Jr. "The Rights of the British Colonies Asserted and Proved." Boston: Edes and Gill, 1764.

Roosevelt, Theodore. "Letter to Henry L. Sprague." January 26, 1900. Presidential Papers, Library of Congress.

Roosevelt, Theodore. "The Strenuous Life." Speech at Hamilton Club, Chicago, April 10, 1899.

Twain, Mark. "The Private History of a Campaign That Failed." *Century Magazine*, December 1885.

"Young Roosevelt Takes Stand Against Corruption." *New York Tribune*, April 8, 1882.

About the Author

Jim Davis has spent over twenty-five years discovering one essential truth: leadership isn't about positions or titles—it's about influence and impact. From church education director to corporate training manager, from federal prison classrooms to Fortune 500 boardrooms, Jim has witnessed firsthand how authentic leadership transforms both individuals and organizations.

As a seasoned speaker and facilitator, Jim's approach breaks from traditional leadership theory by focusing on what he calls "the human element"—the space where trust, communication, and personal accountability intersect. His dynamic, application-based teaching style emerged from a simple observation early in his career: people don't just need more information; they need practical wisdom they can apply immediately.

With a master's degree in leadership from Southwestern University, Jim combines academic insight with real-world experience, having trained leaders across diverse industries and organizations. But his most profound lessons often come from unexpected places, like watching a former inmate grasp the principles of personal accountability or seeing a newly promoted supervisor finally understand the difference between managing tasks and leading people.

As founder of **RYVAL**, a company specializing in leadership development and employee training, Jim helps organizations

177

bridge the gap between potential and performance. His mission remains unchanged: helping others discover their capacity to lead with purpose, communicate with clarity, and create positive change in their spheres of influence.

Today, Jim lives in Currituck, North Carolina, with his wife, Karen, and daughter, Abigail. When he's not developing leaders or speaking to audiences, he's likely crafting new ways to make leadership principles more accessible and actionable for everyone.

Want to connect with Jim? You can reach him at jim@jimdavislive.com or visit his website at jimdavislive.com.

Notes